STRUCK

REAL STORIES FROM FAIRFIELD, CALIFORNIA

Published in Beaverton, Oregon, by Good Catch Publishing.
www.goodcatchpublishing.com
V1.1

Printed in the United States of America

TABLE OF CONTENTS

ACKNOWLEDGEMENTS

I would like to thank Vernon Barker for his vision for this book and Travis DeLuna for his hard work in making it a reality. And to the people of Celebration, thank you for your boldness and vulnerability in sharing your personal stories.

This book would not have been published without the amazing efforts of our Project Manager and Editor, Samantha Jaquez. Her untiring resolve pushed this project forward and turned it into a stunning victory. Thank you for your great fortitude and diligence. Deep thanks to our incredible Editor in Chief, Michelle Cuthrell, and Executive Editor, Jen Genovesi, for all the amazing work they do. I would also like to thank our invaluable Proofreader, Melody Davis, for the focus and energy she has put into perfecting our words.

Lastly, I want to extend our gratitude to the creative and very talented Jenny Randle, who designed the beautiful cover for *Struck: Real Stories from Fairfield, California.*

Daren Lindley
President and CEO
Good Catch Publishing

The book you are about to read
is a compilation of authentic life stories.
The facts are true, and the events are real.
These storytellers have dealt with crisis, tragedy, abuse
and neglect and have shared their most private moments,
mess-ups and hang-ups in order for others to learn and
grow from them. In order to protect the identities of those
involved in their pasts, the names and details of some
storytellers have been withheld or changed.

INTRODUCTION

So many times in our lives, out of nowhere ... *bam*, we're *STRUCK*! Maybe with something that has the potential to take our very breath away, to knock us out or to destroy our lives for good. The stories you will read in this book are true stories from real people who lived it and will give you a firsthand account of how, through their worst adversities, they found hope and help to get back up and truly live again. No matter the circumstances, these brave individuals did not stay defeated. With a beautiful strength, they are able to stand in the midst of their crumbling lives.

May their stories inspire you and give you real answers to life's most difficult questions. For if they can make it, we all can make it. Enjoy these awe-inspiring stories from people just like you from Fairfield, California.

NEVER TOO DIRTY
THE STORY OF JONAH
WRITTEN BY KAREN KOCZWARA

"Should I stab him?" my partner hissed, pulling out his knife.

"I don't give a s***. I don't care what you do," I muttered, glaring down in disgust.

As our victim flailed on the ground, my partner swiftly stabbed him several times. Without looking back, we raced up the hill, leaving the guy bleeding in the dirt. I stumbled in my drunken state, my feet pounding the ground, my heart thudding in my chest as we reached the car.

"Drive, man, drive!" my partner yelled, struggling to catch his breath as we threw open the doors and climbed in.

"What happened, man?" the driver asked, slamming his foot on the gas.

"We stabbed that guy. Bleeding pretty bad. Don't know if we killed him."

Don't know if we killed him. My stomach lurched at his words, and I shuddered. I'd been in plenty of fights and seen plenty of blood during my day. But I'd never actually killed someone before. Deep in my gut, I knew we'd done a terrible, terrible thing. As my conscience kicked in, I grew more sickened over our stupid, hasty actions.

Please, don't let that guy be dead.
Oh, man, don't let him be dead.

கைகைகை

I was born in Indiana, at a military hospital. From a very young age, I learned that the world can be a dark, violent and unforgiving place. At just 2 years old, my sense of security was shattered.

One evening, I stood teetering against the coffee table, my chubby little face just peering over the top. Suddenly, my father flew into the room and charged after my mother, his voice growing loud and angry. His eyes filled with monster-like rage as he grabbed her neck and choked her with his thick bare hands. Frightened, I watched as my mother's face turned crimson red under his grip. She finally managed to pry him off and run away. The memory would remain etched in my mind for the rest of my life, serving as a precursor for the painful years to come.

When I was 3, my parents divorced. My mother moved to Northern California and remarried, taking me and my four siblings with her. I did not like my new stepfather and had no respect for his authority. My mother continually threatened to send me back to my father, and when I was 5 years old, she finally did. She threw me on a plane and sent me back to Indiana. My father and I moved just outside Indianapolis, to an area saturated with poverty, crime and violence. As the only white kid in an African-American neighborhood, I learned how to hold my own among the rowdiest of my peers. But it was the violence in my own home that disturbed me most.

My father began beating me regularly, lashing out in anger when I got in his way. I mimicked his behavior on the playground, where I often picked fights with my classmates.

The teachers caught wind of my unruly actions and hauled me off to be spanked. At home, the cycle of abuse continued. *Why not fight? I'm already getting whooped on at home,* I reasoned.

For the next several years, I hopped back and forth between states, spending time at schools in Indiana and California. While I hoped my mother might stand up for me and show me the affection I craved, she instead looked down on me with disgust. When teachers informed her of my wayward behavior, she gave them permission to spank me.

"I hate you! You're a bad kid! I'm taking you to juvenile hall!" she threatened repeatedly.

"No, please don't take me there!" I pleaded.

"You're a bad kid!"

A bad kid. Well, if that's what everyone thinks I am, I might as well keep acting like one, I figured.

Though I never spent more than a year at the same school, somehow I always did well in my studies. Taking note of my potential, my teachers moved me into the gifted classes, where I thrived. While I rarely studied for my exams, I aced every test.

Sports became my primary outlet. As a misfit white kid amongst a rough crowd, sports helped me gain common ground with my peers. I joined Little League and soon gained a reputation as the best kid on the team. While my mother occasionally came to watch me play, I usually rode my bike by myself to the practices and games. For a few moments, as I flew around the bases, the crowd cheering from the bleachers, I forgot all about my dark, broken world back home. I was not Jonah, the bad kid, but Jonah, the baseball star. And it felt good.

Life with my mother remained unstable. She moved frequently, always hopping from one house to the next. She got a job at a gas station, and I often slept on the cold, hard floor there in the evenings while she worked. She continued to make it clear that I was a nuisance, a failure, a horrible kid. One day, she went missing. When I asked my siblings where she'd gone, they delivered some shocking news.

"She's in a mental hospital. You gave her a nervous breakdown," they informed me.

I put my mother in a mental hospital? Am I really that bad? Her words echoed in my mind, and I felt sick to my stomach.

However, I soon learned the truth. My mother was not in a mental hospital, but in jail. She'd been stealing from the gas station, adjusting the books to cover up her crime.

But she'd finally gotten caught, and now it was time to pay the price. It turned out I wasn't the bad one after all.

Aside from sports, life held little meaning. I rarely went to school and began smoking weed and drinking with my friends. During my freshman year, my friends and I decided to cut class, down a few beers and smoke a couple joints. As we wandered aimlessly down the road, my friend motioned to a tall, fancy building up ahead.

"That's a Catholic church," he whispered. "You know, they drink wine in there. We should bust in and see if they have any."

We snuck inside and discovered, to our good fortune, several bottles of wine in a back room. But before we could polish them off, we got caught, and the church parishioners called our parents. When my mother learned the news, she grew furious.

"That's it, Jonah. You're going back to live with your father in Indiana. I can't take this nonsense anymore," she snapped.

I moved back to Indiana, where my father's abuse only escalated. We moved from the rundown part of town to a double unit in a better part of Indiana, and my father's sister moved next door. One day, after learning I'd cut school, my father unleashed his wrath on me. As I sat in a living room chair, he pressed his knees on both of my arms and beat me profusely, smacking me until my head spun and my nose began to bleed. I fought to keep calm and tried not to cry, knowing any resistance would only make him lash out further.

"What are you doing to that boy?!" My aunt, hearing the beatings from next door, flew into the house and tried to pull my father off of me. The terror in her eyes mirrored the terror I'd seen in my own mother's eyes when I was just a toddler. *You are not safe with this man,* she seemed to say. *Just steer clear of him, or he's going to really hurt you someday.*

My father broke my nose that day, but he also broke my last hope as I realized that no matter where I went, trouble always followed. My father did not love me, my mother did not want me and I had nowhere else to go. *Someday,* I decided with fierce determination, *I'll find my way out of this madness. I'll escape for good, and no one will ever hurt me again.*

At 16, I learned some shocking news. While my father was away in Vietnam with the military years before, my mother had an affair. She discovered not long after that she was pregnant with that man's baby. Though my father was angry, they stayed together, and she gave birth to me. As it turned out, the man who had been dishing out my beatings for years did not even share my blood.

Well, that makes sense, I thought bitterly. *No wonder the guy couldn't stand me. No wonder I could do nothing right in his eyes. No wonder he took all his anger out on me. Well, I'm done with him. I'm done with all of them.*

Searching for some sort of direction and sense of belonging, I decided to check out the military. I marched over to the recruiter's office and learned I could take the GED and receive my high school diploma. I went to an adult school, took a class and aced the GED without studying. The military shipped me to Camp Pendleton in California, where I began boot camp. I hoped to become a combat Marine medic. Being a part of the frontline seemed exciting, and for the first time in a long while, I felt some sort of purpose.

My military career, however, got off to a bad start. Smoking was not allowed in boot camp, but I lit up, anyway, sneaking cigarettes into my bunk. When the commanders found the cigarette butts, they punished everyone, but I quickly stepped up and took the blame.

"It was me," I confessed.

The company tried to put me in positive motivation, hoping that might give me the swift kick in the pants to jumpstart my career. The company commander, a small man, yelled continuously in my face. Trying to keep calm, I replied respectfully, "Sir, I understand you are trying to break us down and build us back up. But is this yelling really necessary?"

After nearly eight weeks of getting myself in trouble, the admiral finally approached me. "Look, do you even want to be here? Do you really want to learn?"

I shrugged. "No," I replied honestly.

"Then it would probably be best if you left."

I agreed, and they released me immediately. I returned to Northern California, found an apartment and met up again with my old friends. Though I dabbled with work, I had a difficult time holding down a job, and eventually, I moved back in with my mother. I spent most of my days drinking, smoking weed and hanging out with gangs. My stint in the military had been short-lived, and I had no idea what to do with the rest of my life.

My oldest sister had managed to graduate high school, the only one in the family to stay in school until graduation. Unlike my tumultuous teenage years, hers had been filled with success. She'd been popular among her peers and had even been crowned prom queen. But my older brother became a pot head, a wrestler and a fighter. My middle sister, eager to escape our dysfunctional home, got married at 16. My younger brother already showed signs of trouble. Though at one time we'd all lived under the same roof, we now scattered like debris after a storm, each a victim of misdirection and neglect.

I immersed myself in the gang lifestyle, robbing people, stealing cars and stereos and beating people up. Life in rough neighborhoods and abusive homes had taught me to be tough. I was a fighter, and violence excited me. With no job, I had plenty of time to rouse up trouble. My partners and I hung out near Hunter Hill rest stop, just a few miles east of Vallejo off the I-80 freeway. There, we targeted the homosexuals or the drunks wandering out of the bars nearby, beating them up and robbing them every chance we got. Like a hungry animal after its prey, I looked forward to my next attack and the momentary adrenaline rush that followed.

I began hanging out with a girl I'd met before going off to boot camp. Though I'd done my fair share of sleeping around, I had never maintained a long-term relationship.

This girl seemed different — sweet, attentive and fun. One day, she grew very sick, and we soon learned her appendix was about to burst. After her appendectomy, I showed up at the hospital to visit her.

"Will you marry me?" I blurted, taking her hand as she lay in the bed recovering.

"Yes!" she replied with as much strength as she could muster.

Her mother disapproved of our relationship and did not want us to marry. At 19 years old, I knew we were both young, but I didn't care. I believed I had found true love and, at last, someone who cared for me. We got married and began a life together, neither of us imagining the drastic turn that life would take just a few months down the road.

One chilly February night, my partner and I downed a few beers and smoked some pot before heading out to stir up trouble. High and drunk, we showed up at the Hunter Hill rest stop. My partner shoved a knife in his pocket and wandered into the dimly lit bathroom to see if he could find anyone to victimize. Moments later, he emerged.

"There's a guy in there, and he wants to take us both on," he said.

I knew what that meant. He'd found a homosexual in there. The guy didn't want to fight — he wanted sex.

We jumped the guy and began to beat him up, tearing at his clothes and shoving him to the ground. The guy struggled to his feet and started to run away, and we charged down the hill after him.

"Give me your shoes!" my partner yelled at the guy.

The guy ripped off his shoes and kept running, while we tore after him. *We've got this guy, no sweat. He can't outrun us. He messed with the wrong people tonight.*

We reached the bottom of the hill, and my partner grabbed the guy and threw him to the ground again. Half naked, the guy glanced up at us, his eyes pleading, his body shaking. We'd done this plenty of times. The homosexual guys made perfect targets because they never reported the attacks. So far, we'd gotten away with everything.

"Should I stab him?" my partner hissed, waving his knife inches from the guy's neck.

I shrugged. "I don't give a s***. I don't care what you do," I muttered, glaring at the guy in disgust.

My partner stabbed the guy several times. We then fled up the hill without looking back. My heart raced as we reached the car where our other partner waited. After climbing in, we breathlessly told him what we'd done. As he careened out of the parking lot, tires screeching, my stomach lurched. For the first time in my life, I felt very, very bad. *We've done something terrible. What if we've killed that poor guy? What if he's dead?*

The next day, I scoured the newspaper, searching for any blurb about a killing at a rest stop. When I didn't find anything, I breathed a sigh of relief. *Okay, maybe he got away. Maybe he's not dead.*

Two days later, my partners and I rented a local motel room, where we planned to spend the night drinking ourselves into oblivion. As we cracked open one beer after another, my mind drifted to the man at the rest stop. I could not stop thinking about him.

"We've gotta go look for that guy. We've gotta find out if he's still there," I told my partners. "I still haven't seen a thing about it in the newspaper, and I've got a bad feeling."

The six of us piled in our cars and drove to the rest stop. We raced down the hill to the spot where my partner had stabbed him, but he was not there. Relief swept through me again. *All right, he's gone. He made it.*

But as I turned to head back up the hill, something stopped me, and I discovered, to my horror, the guy lying in the ditch below.

Oh, God, no. There he is. No. No. He's dead. We really killed him. This is bad.

My partners caught up with me and saw the man lying in the ditch below. "Whoa, you really killed him, man!" they cried.

We headed off to a nearby park, where we tried to figure out what to do next. "I can't believe you! He's dead! That guy's dead!" My partner pulled out a .22 gun on me, his face flaming with anger.

I lunged at him, and we went after each other until the rest of the gang managed to separate us. We sped off toward the motel to cool off and figure out what to do next. My mind raced like a freight train as I processed what we'd done. We'd messed plenty of guys up in our time, but we'd never actually killed anyone. Murder was a far different story than robbery and assault. If we got caught, we could go to prison for life. I gulped hard at the thought, and the words my mother spat out when I was a child came back to me. *You're a bad kid. A bad kid. Well, Mom, you're right. I am a very bad kid.*

I racked my brain, trying to figure out what to do next. My partners paced the floor, all panicked as well. It was only a matter of time before someone reported the man missing. The police would be on our tail in a flash. We had to act fast.

I decided to call up my best friend, Harry. Several years older than me, he was a teacher, and he had a strong faith in God. We'd met when I was 16, and he'd become my first true mentor. He often said things like, "I'm praying for you," which I strangely didn't mind. In a sea of instability, it felt nice to know someone cared about me.

"Harry, man, I'm in trouble," I blurted when he picked up the phone. "I'm gonna go away for a long time. But I just want you to know, I didn't kill him." I hung up before he could ask further questions.

I went home to think things through. A couple days later, my partners showed up at the door.

"We called the police, man. Just wanted to give you a heads-up."

Moments later, I glanced out the window and saw a cop car heading down the street. My heart jumped in my chest, and I grabbed the phone to call my mother, who was playing bingo at the local high school. "Mom, I need to talk to you right now," I said urgently.

"Not now, son. I'm one number away from winning bingo," she replied impatiently.

"Mom, this is really important. I'm in trouble. The cops are after me. I did somethin' real bad."

My mother rushed home. "We've gotta get you out of here, son. The cops are going to find you." She snuck me off to a friend's house to hide and called her lawyer. But her lawyer voiced what we both already knew deep down. I needed to turn myself in.

"You didn't do it, though," my mother protested, her eyes filled with terror as she turned to me.

"But I was there, Mom. I saw it happen. That makes me an accomplice," I croaked, trying to take a deep breath. That night was about to change my life forever. I could not keep running. I needed to face the situation head-on, no matter how ugly it got.

I turned myself in and decided to give a statement, but I lied. "We did get into a fight with that guy at the rest stop, but no one stabbed him," I told the police as coolly as I could.

Next, the police interrogated the driver of the getaway car. Lastly, they interviewed my partner, who had stabbed the guy. They spoke to each of us separately, so we had no idea what the others had said. When they brought me back in, I knew we were in big trouble. Our statements hadn't added up, and we were guilty as charged. Murder felony was a serious offense.

"You can't take me to jail!" I protested. "I have claustrophobia!"

But the police didn't care. They hauled me off to Vallejo County Jail, where I would spend the next several months. The place was filled with guys from the roughest parts of the street. On the way over, I threw out a prayer to God, asking him to keep me safe.

"God, if you get me out, I will serve you, I promise," I told him. I had not spoken to God much in my life, but I figured if he did exist, it was best to take a chance on him. After all, I had nothing left at the moment.

I called my wife and told her what had happened. Just before the incident, she'd told me that she thought she was pregnant. I was eager to find out how she was doing.

"Jonah, I have some bad news. I lost the baby," she told me, her voice cracking with emotion.

"Oh, man." My heart sank. Despite my messed-up ways, I had been looking forward to being a father. It broke me to think that she'd lost our child.

The divorce papers arrived shortly after, and our whirlwind marriage came to an abrupt end. My wife did not want to be married to a guy who was facing a possible life term in prison for murder. And in my gut, I did not blame her. I had ruined my life, but she was not about to let me take her down, too.

I spent the next eight months in jail, reading the Bible from front to back four times. While a couple guys tried to mess with me, most left me alone. I hunkered down on my bunk, praying to God every night. "Please, God, get me out of this."

And then, October 17, 1989, an earthquake rattled the

jail. I jumped out of my bunk, terrified as the entire building violently shook. *I gotta get outta here. I can't die in this place. I just can't. God, help me. I'll do anything for you. Just get me out.*

I soon learned that the earthquake was a 6.9 magnitude that killed dozens of people and injured thousands more. It struck during warm-up practice for game three of the World Series between the Oakland Athletics and the San Francisco Giants, causing mayhem in the Bay Area and beyond. But it also shook my own little world, in which I was growing more claustrophobic by the day. I called my friends and begged them to get the bail money together to get me out of jail. They did, and after spending eight long months behind bars, I was finally released.

With a trial still looming, I knew I wasn't really a free man. But I decided to live it up the best I could, making the most of the fresh air while it lasted. Instead of going to church like I'd promised God I'd do, I headed straight to the bars, where I picked up women and drank the night away. With my clean-cut look, people mistook me for a military guy, and I played along with it.

I was soon taken back into custody. Again, I hit my knees, praying harder than I ever had before. I read a poem called "Footsteps," in which the author described Jesus carrying us through trials.

"Carry me, please, God," I begged him. I picked up my Bible and flipped through it, desperate for his help. "God, please, help me!" I used him like a lifeline, holding on to

STRUCK

the end of the rope in hopes that he would pull me up before it was too late.

I learned I'd be going to New Folsom State Prison, one of the most violent prisons in the state. I was scared to death. I'd heard horror stories about the place and knew the guys there meant business. If I did not conjure a game plan immediately, I'd be sucked in and trampled by them. I decided the only thing to do was to pretend I was not afraid. I'd march in, act tough and show them who was boss. *If I'm top dog, no one will mess with me.*

I showed up at the prison and took over the yard, joining up with a black gang. My little plan worked, and no one messed with me. I quickly learned the ropes in the system. If someone initiated a fight, you had to stab him or he would kill you. There was no other option.

Feeling hopeless, I concluded that the best plan of action was not to keep fighting for my life, but to kill myself. I fashioned a noose out of my sheet and tied it to a nearby locker. I then slipped the noose around my neck. I deduced that if I raised my legs up and held my ankles, the noose would tighten around my neck, and I would die. It seemed like the perfect way to end the madness before it began.

To my disappointment, however, the noose broke. I flopped back down on the bed, defeated. *I can't even kill myself. This sucks. I guess I'm stuck here in this hell for now.*

I learned I would be transferred over to Old Folsom State Prison. The second-oldest prison in California next

to San Quentin, it had seen its fair share of executions since the state introduced the death penalty. It is best known for Johnny Cash's performance of "Folsom Prison Blues" behind its doors in the 1960s. And I was headed there.

"Congratulations, your parole officer was probably born today," folks said when I arrived. I knew what they meant — I was never going to get out.

The guards locked me up in a cell on the main line. The unit included five tiers, each with a cement sidewalk roughly 3 feet wide.

My cell was comprised of a bunk, toilet, sink and storage space. Two dining halls, a large central prison exercise yard, two smaller yards and a visiting room with an attached patio made up the rest of the facility. All day long, the sound of slamming bars and yelling echoed up and down the halls.

I was the youngest guy on the main line, surrounded by guys who had been in for years and had little to no chance of getting out. Not long after arriving, a guy approached me with a syringe full of drugs. Though I'd smoked plenty of weed in my lifetime, I'd never put a needle in my arm. After trying to get me to use the needle with him, the guy made a pass at me. Angry, I yanked him up and tried to fit him in between the cell bars. I'd learned that men in prison made passes at each other to show that they "owned" the other person. I wanted to make it abundantly clear to this guy that he would never own me or make a pass at me again. In the future, I'd have to play it cool and learn how to play the game without offending anyone or getting killed or raped.

I went out on the yard and met the shot caller of the Blood gang. I had seen him around and told him who I was.

"Look, man, we'll stand with you, but you should go to your own people. You are already a man of position in Vacaville. If you wanna be with us, we'll fight with you, but the white guys are gonna come get you. I'm not allowed to turn you away, but if you stay with us, you're gonna be trouble."

"All right, man, I see what you're sayin'. I'll take your advice and go to my own people." *So this is how it works around here.* I'd been so accustomed to hanging around black guys, I often forgot I wasn't one of them. I wandered back inside, carefully plotting my next move. Reputations spread quickly around this place, and if I didn't establish myself, I could be in big trouble.

During shower time, someone hollered to me, "Hey, Jonah, 'Extra-Large' wants to see you!"

"Extra-Large" was the barber in our unit. I headed over to see what he had to say.

"Man, I know you just got here. I saw you walkin' laps with that n*****, and we thought for sure you were gonna fight that guy. What are you thinkin'?"

"Don't worry. I'm gonna stay with my own people," I quickly replied.

Within no time, I learned the rest of the prison lingo and makeshift rules. Because I'd walked laps with a black guy, the other gangs decided to "DP," or discipline me. This ritual was based on the 23rd letter of the alphabet, W, which stood for White. Guys who were "DP'd" were forced to fight for 23 seconds. After my first round, I learned that I was supposed to let them beat me without fighting back. I didn't like that, as I wanted to get mine in, too. But if I was going to make it in here, I'd have to play the game their way.

My case went to trial, and I was sentenced to 25 years to life in prison. I called up my mother, crying, but learned she was in jail, too.

"I'm gonna be home in a year and a half," she told me. "You hang in there, son."

My mother met a girl in jail who'd been locked up for switching price tags at stores to make money. She encouraged me to write her, and I agreed to. After communicating back and forth, the girl and I decided to get married.

After getting out of jail, she came to visit me. Not long after, she announced she was pregnant. Nine months later, our beautiful daughter arrived. I was now a father, something I'd always wanted to be, yet I could not provide for my little one the way I wanted to. I hoped things would one day change. Perhaps if God issued me a second chance and got me out, I could make a decent life for my new family.

As the days passed, my anxiety grew worse. One night, as I lay in bed, I felt as if an arm reached across my back and squeezed my heart. Panic seized me as I realized I must be having a heart attack. I lay there, muttering the Lord's Prayer, waiting to die. I had never felt such excruciating pain in all my life.

Finally, the pain subsided for a moment, and I was able to breathe. A cop had been pacing the floor, as we were on lockdown. He stopped at my cell, and when he saw me doubled over in pain, he took me to the nurse's station. But after checking my vitals, she deemed me perfectly fine.

"You just had an anxiety attack," she determined.

The cop marched me back to my cell, and I picked up my Bible and began to flip through the pages. I then hit my knees and threw out several desperate prayers. "God, I don't want to die in prison. Please, help me. I'm so scared."

I prayed daily, hoping that if God really did exist, he would hear my prayers. I knew I'd been a terrible person, but I hoped that despite my selfishness, he might throw a little mercy my way. Sometimes, I fell asleep on my knees praying, waking on the cold, hard floor in the morning. I did not care who saw me pray — it was my only hope, the only thing that kept me going in otherwise bleak circumstances.

I was transferred to the lower level 3 security unit soon after, and I breathed a sigh of relief. Compared to the violent world I'd just left, the place was like an amusement park. I was now able to play sports and participate in other recreational activities. No longer in immediate danger, I decided I didn't need my Bible anymore. God had served his purpose for the time being, and now I could put him back on the shelf.

I moved again down to level 2 and landed a job as a family visiting clerk. Because I was smart, the work came easily to me, and I succeeded at my tasks. The job also provided a way for me to see my wife and daughter more frequently. They came often for visits, and I was amazed to see how much my daughter had grown. When the prison took the family visits away a couple years later, I decided I no longer wanted the job. My wife and I began fighting, and I learned she was heavily involved in drugs and being unfaithful. I asked for a divorce, and she finally relented. With two failed marriages under my belt, I wondered if I'd ever find a good woman again.

For the next several years, I worked my way into the best jobs available at the prison. In just five short weeks, with only 20 lessons on CD, I taught myself Braille. The inmates and officers were all amazed, as they'd never seen anyone learn something so quickly. I thought back to my high school days, when I'd aced all of my exams without studying. *Perhaps I really am smart, and perhaps I still do have a future ahead of me. Maybe I can still contribute in a meaningful way.*

I continued to see my daughter every weekend, but when my prison turned into a level 3, I was moved to Avenal in King's County several hours away. I'd now only be able to see my daughter every six to eight months. The arrangement broke my heart, but I vowed to keep in touch as frequently as possible so I did not miss out on her life.

The head of education called me one day with a proposition. "We heard you are trained in Braille, and we want to know if you will open up a Braille class on a different yard."

I hesitated to say yes. The guys on my yard had become like family, and I had a great rapport with them. I'd fought hard to get where I was and was content with my current circumstances. "I'll think about it," I told her.

She called back again with the same proposition. "I'll do it, but I want a dollar an hour," I said firmly. In prison currency, a dollar an hour was a substantial amount of money. She agreed to it, and we had ourselves a deal.

I moved to the other yard, taking my drugs with me. I'd learned the oldest drug-smuggling trick in the book to avoid getting caught by the cops — stuffing them up my butt. I was prepared to set up shop at the new yard and carry on with business. The guys were aware I was coming, and I knew I'd have plenty of buyers in no time.

When I arrived at the new yard, the rain began to come down in a torrent, and the chilly air whipped at my cheeks. I quickly realized I did not have my gate pass and could not get in the yard. Angry, I decided to head into the chapel to stay dry. I sat down and listened as an inmate preached from the front of the room.

"It is okay to tell God how angry you are," he said. "In the Bible, a man named David did this, pouring out his feelings to God as his enemies pursued him. You may be sitting here today full of anger because of the circumstances in your life. It is okay to say, 'I am angry because my mom has cancer. I am angry because things haven't gone the way I wanted. I am angry because I am sick.' God hears your prayers, and he can handle them. He understands. I've been angry plenty of times, and I just tell God how I feel. It's okay. He cares. He isn't going anywhere. He still loves you."

I sat frozen in my seat, struck by his words. *That's me! I am angry! Angry because I grew up in a dysfunctional home. Angry because a guy I thought was my father beat me for years. Angry because just when things seem to be going right, they all fall apart. I am angry!*

But beyond my anger, I dared to believe something else — something wonderful. Something that almost seemed too good to be true. God cared for me. He loved me. He was prepared to handle my grief, my problems, my sorrow, my pain. He was big enough. I only needed to surrender my life to him.

As the inmate prayed, I prayed along with him, asking God to wipe my slate clean. *God, I know I've messed up really badly. I've prayed to you many times out of desperation, but I've never truly given my heart to you. I ask you to come into my heart right now. Please forgive me for the wrong I've done, and help me to live for you. I need you. I get it now. You're my only hope, the only one who can change me from the inside out.*

After the message was over, I walked up to the guy and shook his hand. "You changed a life today," I told him with a smile.

I walked out of that little chapel feeling lighter and

freer than I ever had in my life. Suddenly, all of the pieces fit together, making perfect sense. I'd read the Bible from front to back several times and could even quote several texts. I had all the knowledge, but I'd never let it penetrate my heart. I'd thrown out prayers to God over the years, pleading with him to protect me, help me and save me. I'd used him like a lifeline, then shoved him back on the shelf when I felt I didn't need him anymore.

But in the process, I'd missed the entire point. God was not some good-luck genie I needed to rub to avoid bad things from happening. Instead, he was the creator of the universe, the one who had known my name before I was even born, the only one who loved me 100 percent unconditionally. The purpose of praying and reading the Bible was to grow closer to him, not to pick up a few pieces of good fortune along the way. God wanted a relationship with me. He'd wanted that all along, but I wasn't ready. I'd been too busy living for myself, trying to do things my way. Now, I saw it all differently. He had opened my heart to receive his love, and I now fully embraced it.

I'm ready, God. I want this new life. I'm done with the old way. Thank you, God!

I took all my drugs and flushed them down the toilet. When I walked out to the yard, a guy approached me.

"I need some weed, man. I hear you got some."

"I am done with that," I replied.

"You're f***ing with me," he snapped. "Where's the dope?"

"I flushed it."

His face grew red with anger. "Are you kidding me? I had buyers for that."

"Sorry." I shrugged. "I'm a Christian now."

"Wait a sec. So you're a Christian now?"

"Yep. I found Jesus."

"Well, you better stay that way, or we're comin' for you."

As he stormed off, I nearly chuckled aloud. I understood his skepticism. I'd met many guys in prison who'd claimed to follow Jesus, yet they weren't any different than anyone else.

I intended to prove to them that I was. I would be that 100 percent real Jesus follower from now on, and I would send the message loud and clear that I didn't want any more drugs sent my way.

From that moment on, things changed. God opened my eyes to the Christian community at the prison, and within no time, I met many other guys who genuinely loved God.

We spent our days doing everything together, from watching movies to chatting to playing sports to attending Bible studies. We held church in the yard, on the bleachers or anywhere else we could gather. Even the rain did not stop us from meeting. We were inseparable.

To my surprise, we quickly gained favor in the yard. We made it clear who we were and what we believed in and informed our fellow inmates that if they tried to fight with us, we would not fight them. Instead of picking fights, they watched us, wanting what we had. Soon, guys of all races, sizes and backgrounds approached us with curiosity.

"Trust me. I've been around a while, and I've seen a lot of stuff. Following God is the best way," I told them. "You are never too dirty for God to clean you up."

As more men continued to hang out with us and attend the Bible studies, I grew excited. For the first time in my entire life, I had what felt like a real family. I had a place to belong, a place where other like-minded guys loved me, a place to be accepted. Many of them had come from harsh backgrounds like me, but thanks to God, they now experienced the same peace, hope and joy I'd found. To an outsider, we were just a bunch of guys in prison jumpsuits hanging in the yard, but to us, we were a tight-knit family of believers in Jesus Christ, and our bond could not be broken.

As my first possible release date approached, I grew excited about the idea of going home. But I wasn't as anxious to be released now. Though still technically behind bars, I already felt free.

In 2010, I went before the board, and they denied me for release. After talking with my buddy, he suggested I appeal their decision. I gathered my transcripts, and he helped me put in my appeal.

"The court has to justify why they are keeping you in prison," he said. "If they don't have a good enough reason, they need to let you go."

The court came back with a release date of 2016.

Okay, six more years. Not the end of the world. At least I won't be spending the rest of my life in here.

As I continued to grow in my new faith, I began to pray also for a godly woman. *How awesome would it be to meet a woman who loves God! It would be so great to share that connection, just like I have with my fellow inmates!*

I met a woman online, and we began chatting. When I learned we shared the same beliefs, I was thrilled. Though she lived on the East Coast, we committed to a long-distance relationship until I got out of prison. We married on January 15, 2011, and I thanked God for answering my prayers in a way I never could have imagined. He had truly given me the desire of my heart.

That same year, I learned some devastating news. My daughter, now in her late teens, had been prostituting herself out and advertising online. My heart sank at the news. It crushed me to think of all the time I'd missed with her over the years. I prayed, asking God to release her of this destructive lifestyle. I knew she must be lost and hurting, wandering in the wildness as I had for years. I hoped she would one day discover the wonderful, loving God I had and want a relationship with him, too.

I went before the courts again, and they moved my release date up to 2014. I was happy. In the meantime, I stuck close to my brothers in the yard, never faltering in my faith. Men of all backgrounds continued to approach us, asking about our faith. I was happy to tell them about a God of second chances, a God who had taken my messed-up life and turned it around. As I spoke, I watched their eyes flicker with hope. It was the same hope I'd found when I walked in the doors of that chapel and heard that inmate speak. This wasn't some feel-good drug that would wear off in a few hours. This was the real deal, and those who discovered it never looked back.

With my extra time, I developed two programs to be used in the education system. BEAR stood for Become Educated And Responsible. Local high schools brought kids into the prison to see me, and I shared openly about the struggles behind bars.

"You want to stay out of trouble, because if you don't, you could find yourself in some pretty harsh conditions," I warned the kids. "So stick with a good crowd, stay away from drugs and stay in school."

I also developed The PROGRAM, educating parents about the signs of gang activity and what to look for in their own children. Both churches and schools soon learned about my programs and wanted me to implement them at their facilities. I was flattered but gave God all the credit. He had given me a good mind and the ability to put that mind to use in a positive way.

When I presented my material at my progress hearing, the parole commissioners raved about it.

"This could really flourish in the prison system," they agreed. "This is a really great thing you've done."

Due to my excellent behavior and my standout programs, the court moved up my release date again. I called my new wife with the good news.

"I'm going to be released soon! I can't wait to see you!" I told her excitedly. I smiled, picturing her pretty face in my mind. Sometimes I still had to pinch myself to believe she was real. God had truly brought me a godly woman who loved me just as I was. Soon, we'd be united in person, and the celebration could begin.

My wife flew out to be with me when I was released. But that release date was delayed by two weeks, forcing us to wait even longer to be united.

On June 19, 2013, I walked out of prison for good. My mother, stepfather, sister, wife and daughter greeted me at the gate. We embraced, enjoying a beautiful reunion together. I was free at last.

༄༅༄༅

Though I praised God for working such a miracle in my life, my release was bittersweet. I was beyond grateful to be free, but I'd also developed some amazing, tight-knit friendships behind bars.

I would never forget my inmates and our time together. I knew how important it was to stick with a group of people who loved God, and I was determined to find that when I got home.

I returned to Northern California and decided to check out two or three churches before settling on one. My sister suggested I visit Celebration Church.

At the end of the first service I attended there, the pastor gave an altar call, asking anyone who would like to come forward for prayer to step up. I flew out of my seat and made my way toward the front, where the tears came in a flood.

Thank you, God. Oh, thank you, for taking a guy like me and turning my life around. You have done a true miracle in my heart, and I am truly speechless.

A week later, I returned to Celebration Church.

"I was going to visit some other churches, but I don't want to. I know I've found a place to call home," I told the pastor.

"Well, welcome home," he said with a smile.

That summer, I dove into the Bible studies at church, eager to meet new people and get involved. Everyone embraced me with love, treating me like family. Once again, I thanked God for bringing me to just the right place. He had truly brought my life full circle.

Since leaving prison, I've thought long and hard about my life. I am now a free man, not just physically, but spiritually and emotionally, as well. God took my dirty, messed-up life and transformed it into something amazing.

As a kid, I believed I was bad, that I was nothing but a troublesome nuisance. As a teenager, I lived up to those words. And as a young adult, I lived an aimless, empty life, soon joining the worst of the worst. But it was in the darkest prison that God rescued me. He took the gunk, wiped me clean and reminded me that I was never too dirty for him to clean up. Now I had a chance to remind others of that.

NEVER TOO DIRTY

While I long ago forgave my mother for everything, I still pray that she, as well as my daughter, would discover the Jesus I've been introduced to. In him, I have a renewed sense of hope and, with it, a reason to start living again.

LOVE NEVER FAILS
THE STORY OF VIVIAN
WRITTEN BY KAREN KOCZWARA

I just want to die.

I threw myself on the living room floor, exhausted, angry and completely defeated. The tears came in a flood, unstoppable as they cascaded down my face and trickled onto the carpet.

God, this isn't fair! I'm trying my hardest here! I don't know what to do! I have nowhere to go. I have no job, no food and two kids. I've lived my whole life trying to please everyone around me! Who the h*** worries about me? Who takes care of me?

The years of pain and fighting had caught up to me. I had nothing left to give. Nothing left to live for. Except my two precious children.

I thought of little Renee and David, tucked into their beds and sleeping peacefully upstairs. The children I wasn't sure I wanted to have. They were now my whole world. And as difficult as things were, I had to stay alive for them. Somehow, we would escape this mess and find better days ahead.

Oh, God, there have to be better days ahead. I just can't keep going on this way!

STRUCK

❧❧❧

I was born in 1975 in Northern California. My younger brother, Ramon, followed three years later. My father was an angry man who beat my mother and brother down with his hurtful words. He favored me over my brother, often referring to Ramon as a wimp because of the young boy's tendency to get sick. But Ramon still looked up to my father, hoping he might become pleasing in his eyes. He shoved my father's t-shirts and pillow into his backpack and toted them to school, wanting to catch a whiff of my father's familiar scent. I instinctively learned to protect my brother, knowing we both faced a difficult and often cruel world.

One day, as I rode with my father and little 4-year-old Ramon in the car, Ramon murmured something that upset my father. My father slammed on the brakes and stopped the car in the middle of the street. He then whirled around and threw his hands up, attempting to hit Ramon in the face.

"Stop it!" I screamed, terror ripping through me. "Stop hitting my brother!"

"Shut up, or you'll get the same," my father snarled.

I slumped into the seat, fighting back tears. *Why is Dad always so angry? What did we do to make him so mad?*

My father's temper soon took a toll on my mother, and she crumbled. In her hurt, she struggled to show love and affection to me. She began to hurl angry words my way, insisting I had an "attitude" all the time. "You are just like your father!" she often cried.

Perhaps I really am a bad kid, I decided sadly.

I sought refuge with a woman named May. In her early 50s, May lived across the street from my ailing grandmother, whom my mother often cared for. May loved me like a daughter, and I grew to care for her like a mother. She often let me sleep over and set aside a room in her house for my toys and personal belongings. But while her house became a haven, it soon became a place of terror, as well.

At night, May laid out a little sleeping bag for me right next to her bed. One night, I awakened to find myself between May and her husband, Bruce. His clothes were off, and immediately, I shuddered. Though just a little girl, I knew something wasn't right.

The following year, Bruce began taking pictures of me as I bathed in May's tub. When he entered the bathroom, I quickly flipped over onto my stomach and covered my bottom with a washcloth, ashamed to let him see me. Other times, he motioned me into the den and showed me his *Playboy* magazines. I cringed, not interested in peeking at the scantily clad women between the pages. I decided to stick close to May, never wanting to leave her side. When she showered, I sat by the bathroom door and cried, afraid to be alone with Bruce. I just knew something didn't feel right.

In elementary school, I spent the night at a close friend's house. In the middle of the night, her father stormed through the house in a drunken rage, yelling and screaming. I trembled under my covers, terrified, while the rest of the family slept through the noise. Later, I slept over at another friend's house, and her father unleashed his fury on his children and beat them. The screaming echoed in my head for days, and I decided I was done with sleepovers. *No matter where I go, there's some sort of chaos. Nowhere is safe.*

In my own home, my father's hurtful words continued to fly. My mother marched my brother and me to church every Sunday and often prayed for my father to come with us. I attended Sunday school classes, but the routine meant little to me. I played under the pews and giggled, not paying much attention to the message. *Abuse at home, and God on Sundays. This is just the way things are around here.*

My mother often threatened to leave my father. When I was 10, he finally relented and went to church with us. From then on, he changed his ways. His anger died down, but in its place, my mother's rose up. Her spirit had been crushed years ago, and she now bore her own set of scars. She often lashed out at me, threatening me with her words and actions. Once, she sat on me and shoved oatmeal down my throat, knowing full well I hated the mushy stuff. Another time, she wrestled a bar of soap into my mouth. I grew to believe I was as awful as she insisted I was.

I retreated to May's house, where I was always welcomed by her with a warm hug and a smile. Bruce

LOVE NEVER FAILS

continued to make me uncomfortable, exposing himself to me and insisting I sit on his shoulders while he watched TV.

"You know you will never see May again if you tell your parents what happens here," Bruce whispered, his tone kind but firm.

I kept his advances to myself, not wanting to lose the only person who seemed to find value in me.

When I got in trouble with my mother, she refused to let me go to May's house. Devastated, I sat in my grandmother's window and glanced across the street, letting the tears fall. If there was one thing I was certain of, it was May's love.

Fear and anxiety plagued me wherever I went. Panic attacks and stomach issues soon followed, and I often feared I might vomit. I wound up in the hospital several times with stomach issues. When I grew sick, my father ran down to 7-Eleven and returned with a bottle of Pepto-Bismol. I quickly downed the stuff, hoping it would keep my nausea at bay. From then on, the pink liquid became my security blanket, and I made sure I had it in my backpack at all times.

One day, while all the other kids went to recess, my teacher, Mr. Black, saw me sitting on the steps alone and approached me. I'd always admired his kindness and love toward his family and knew I could trust him. As we began to talk, I opened up to him.

"Are you saved?" he asked.

"I don't know what that means," I replied.

"Do you believe in God?"

"Of course." I'd been in church for years, heard all the Bible stories and sang all the songs. I definitely believed in God.

"Then, do you want to invite Jesus into your heart?" he pressed.

"Yes!"

Mr. Black led me through a prayer, and I invited Jesus into my heart right there on those school steps. I went home, excited about something for the first time in a long while. *I belong to someone! He loves me, and I love him!* It was a wonderful feeling, much like the warmth I experienced when May wrapped me in a long hug. *I have Jesus now!*

But life did not ease up. Just as my adolescent hormones kicked in, two cousins molested me, taking advantage of me while the adults gathered in another room. Another piece of me died that day, and I wondered again if I really was as worthless and awful as everyone said. One thing was for certain — I was determined to steer clear of men at all costs. They were nothing but trouble.

When I was in the sixth grade, May grew sick and passed away. I attended her funeral — it was the first I'd ever been to. I sobbed uncontrollably, wrought with grief over losing a woman I'd come to care for like flesh and blood. She'd provided love, relief and refuge in the midst of my tumultuous life, and I wasn't sure how I'd go on without her.

Bruce moved away and kept the belongings I'd stored at May's house. After her death, my world completely fell apart. I retreated to the corner of my bedroom and rocked back and forth until sleep beckoned. My anxiety worsened, and fearing I might throw up, I decided to alleviate the pain another way. I started cutting myself, using the sharp tip of a pen cap to dig into my upper thighs. I covered the jagged marks with my clothing, just as I masked the hurt in my heart with a forced smile for the world.

My grades, once all A's and B's, plummeted after May's death. I decided I no longer cared about school or anything else. Though I remained close to my cousin Marie, I kept everyone else at a distance. While friendly to my peers, I refused to let anyone in. *Best to not get close to anyone. Best to stay away so they don't hurt me, too.* Loneliness ate at me, and deep inside, I longed for a best friend. But I was too broken to open my heart to anyone.

My pain grew into anger. I began to lash out at everyone, just as my parents had at me. Before long, I had the very "attitude" my mother insisted I did. One day, just before the bell rang in class, I chatted with a friend. My teacher marched up to me with a bottle of Windex and promptly sprayed it in my face.

"Stop talking!" the teacher barked.

I stared at him, stunned, as I wiped the liquid from my cheeks. *Did he really just do that in front of everyone?*

I told my father about the incident, and he grew furious and marched down to the school to report the

STRUCK

teacher's actions. The next day, my teacher came to school in tears, so shaken he could barely instruct the class.

"I really want to apologize for what I did, Vivian. I'm so sorry," he said.

I sank into my seat, mortified that my father had dealt with him. *Now the whole school will know,* I thought miserably. *It seems no matter where I go, trouble always seems to ensue.*

When high school rolled around, my mother asked me where I wanted to go. I had attended a Christian school thus far, and she remained adamant that I continue at a Christian school.

I wanted to go to a Catholic school downtown that was an all-girls school, which appealed to me. *I won't have to deal with any drama there. Plus, everyone wears uniforms, so I won't have to worry about dressing up to impress anyone.*

I liked my new school well enough, and my grades improved significantly. But inside, I remained a broken little girl, masking my pain with anger and indifference. When summer arrived, I landed a job at a local water park. When my parents decided on a trip to Disneyland with my brother, they told me I'd have to stay behind with my grandmother.

"You're working, so you can't come," they said.

Practically, that may have been true. But it felt like rejection. I loved my little brother deeply and had spent years fiercely trying to protect him in his frail, sickly state. Our family had always been chaotic and disjointed, and

I'd never quite felt like I'd belonged. Now that I was nearing adulthood, I realized we were all victims in our own way, each reeling from our pain and trying to find our place in the world. I wondered if we'd ever find harmony and peace, or if we'd spend the rest of our lives hurting and misunderstanding each other.

I befriended several guys at work who treated me with respect, as a big brother would. One day, my 26-year-old male boss called me into his office and began pressing me with questions.

"Do you have a boyfriend?" he asked.

I shook my head shyly, disgusted by his advances. *This guy is 10 years older than me! Why is he bugging me?*

At last, I decided that if he wanted to play the romantic game, I could play it right back. I used my charm to manipulate him into assigning me the areas I wanted to work. *Stupid guys. They're all the same,* I thought, rolling my eyes.

Several of my guy friends worked as bouncers at the local clubs. I told my parents I was spending the night at a friend's house, then slipped out to the clubs, using my fake ID to get in. Many of the guys did drugs as well, and I hung out with them as they chopped up cocaine with a razorblade and packed it for sale. My friends, always protective of me, would not let me near them while they "worked." I had no interest in doing drugs. Deep down, I knew it was wrong. But hanging out at their houses was better than spending time at home.

I met a guy named Ray, and we began dating. I lost my

virginity to him, and immediately, my conscience gnawed at me. Growing up in church, I knew right from wrong, and I did not want to displease God. I confided in my aunt, who insisted I tell my mother. I told both my parents, and though my father's face registered disappointment, my mother's registered disdain.

"I knew you were a slut since the day you were born," she said, rolling her eyes. "Get in the car. We're going to Ray's house."

Mortified, I watched as my father and mother sped off to Ray's house, where she was about to confront the young boy and his mother. The family was not home, and to my relief, my parents returned. Unfortunately, Ray's family came over to my house. His mother barked at Ray when she heard the news, admonishing him for his stupid behavior. I ran outside in tears, and Ray's little brother tried to comfort me.

"It's okay. Please don't cry," he said softly. "My mom's always yelling."

I wanted to sink into the ground and never resurface. *No matter what I do or where I go, I always make trouble. I must be a really bad kid,* I thought, shame seeping into my heart.

The summer before my senior year, I met a sweet guy named Ben at the water park. Unlike many of the guys at school, Ben was completely respectful and treated me like a princess.

We spent the entire summer together, and at the beginning of my senior year, though he had already graduated, he picked me up for school every morning and drove me to class. Slowly, I opened my heart to him.

One weekend, he did not call me as usual. *That's not like him,* I thought, slightly worried. *Ben is always completely attentive.*

On Monday morning, he picked me up for school. The moment I saw his face, I immediately knew something was wrong. My stomach lurched as we drove in silence. As we approached the school, Ben handed me a letter without looking at me.

"What's this?" I asked, my voice barely above a whisper.

"Please, don't open it right now," he begged. "You better go now, Vivian." Though he avoided my eyes, I knew he was crying.

Ignoring his request to wait, I grabbed the letter and read it at that moment. He had written to inform me he was enlisting in the military and would be leaving for boot camp in two weeks. *I can't be with you,* he wrote. *A relationship wouldn't work with the Marine lifestyle. I'm so sorry.*

You've gotta be kidding me, I thought, my heart sinking to the ground. I had been so certain Ben was different, that our relationship had what it took to last. I'd pictured myself married to him. We'd even discussed that if he ever did leave for the military, I would go with him. How could he do this to me right now?

After he pleaded with me to get out of the car, I stepped out, hurt and angry. I walked down the street in a daze, so devastated I didn't care if I got hit by a car. *So this is what it feels like to have a broken heart. It physically hurts, like it's twisting in my chest. My first real love, and now it's gone. Just like that. I'll never get over this as long as I live.*

I continued to make trouble at school, always speaking out in class and smarting back to my teachers. My poor behavior got me kicked off the cheer squad.

"Vivian, can you please be quiet?" my teacher asked one day, his patience growing thin.

"Why do I have to be quiet?" I snapped, rolling my eyes. I now felt like a ticking time bomb, just waiting to explode. Though petite, I was ready to take on anyone who glanced at me the wrong way. *Bring it on! You wanna mess with me, I'll mess right back!*

I began cutting class, no longer interested in my studies. Deep down, the pain gnawed at me, a festering wound that never healed. I did not have the words to shout, "See me! I am broken! I am hurting!" I could only shout in anger and take a stab at others before they injured me.

I continued cutting myself to bleed out the pain. Meanwhile, my stomach issues persisted, and I developed an ulcer. Six months before graduation, I got kicked out of school for my poor behavior. My mother, desperate to see me get my diploma, begged the school to keep me, but they insisted on letting me go. I began classes at a public school, and from the moment I set foot on campus, I sensed the principal did not like me.

"Girls who come from those private schools are always snobby," the principal muttered.

Though my new school presented its own set of challenges, I met a nice boy named John. He was goofy and fun to be around. Though I was not attracted to him, I appreciated his kindness, and my family took a liking to him as well. Even when I preferred not to be in class, he made going to school a little bit better.

Just as I felt I was finally able to get on with my life, Ben returned from boot camp.

We had not spoken in months, and I had no idea he was home. He showed up at my school to pick me up, but I was not there because I was cutting class. Later that day, I saw him at the mall and learned that he came searching for me. A glimmer of hope sparked in my heart. That hope only grew larger when we became intimate after dinner that night.

At first I refused his advances. "You said you would only be with the woman you want to marry!"

"And I still feel that way," he said. I melted at his words and gave in to the hope that we could be together forever. At the end of our whirlwind weekend, he went back to boot camp. Little did I know that when he came to look for me at my school, he met another girl instead. That girl would eventually become his wife, and any dreams of the two of us reuniting would be flushed away for good. What little trust I had for men completely disappeared, and I decided I absolutely could not give my heart away to anyone again.

I continued going to clubs and cutting class. After mouthing off to more teachers at my new school, I got kicked out of there as well, with just two months to go until graduation. *I guess no school can handle a smart-mouthed girl like me,* I realized, convincing myself I no longer cared.

I discussed my anxiousness with my friend John, to get out of my house, and he suggested I come live with him and his mother. Reluctantly, I moved in with them, but after just a couple months, he announced that he, too, was joining the military.

Immediately, I grew angry. Memories of Ben, my first real love, flooded my mind. I hated the Marines, because they had robbed me of my future with him. I watched John go, and he insisted I stay with his mother while he was gone. Though the living situation was awkward, I reasoned it was better than living under my parents' roof.

When John returned from boot camp, I agreed to go with his mother to the graduation ceremony. The moment I saw him in his sharp Marine uniform, my heart did a little flip. *Whoa, who is this guy? He looks amazing!* John had lost weight and hardly resembled the guy who had left three months before. After the ceremony, we met up.

"How are you, Vivian?" he asked, looking at me fondly.

"Pretty good. You?"

"Well, I thought about you the whole time I was gone," he confessed. "I kept your senior picture with me, and it helped me survive boot camp."

This guy really likes me. He's not talking to me like a friend anymore.

"Vivian, I really wish you would be with me. Like, all the time."

The idea frightened me, but it didn't seem like the end of the world, either.

My mother loved John, and I was still desperate to please her. Plus, John could provide a stable home environment. I was lonely and craved companionship. Perhaps we could make the arrangement work.

"I'll be with you, but I'm only doing this to get away from my parents," I told him honestly.

"It's okay. I get it. I want to take care of you."

After months of this living situation, John asked me to marry him. Though I was reluctant, I agreed. We decided to tie the knot at a little chapel in Reno. As all of our friends and family gathered to celebrate, dread filled my insides. I knew I didn't love John as more than a friend, and this was hardly the fairytale wedding most little girls dreamed about. It was a marriage of convenience, nothing more.

John secured me an apartment and gave me access to his bank account. The Marines sent him away, and I began inviting friends over, enjoying my newfound freedom. *Maybe this isn't so bad after all,* I decided.

But after a while, guilt gnawed at me. I knew John had a good heart, and I felt bad stringing him along.

When he returned home, I said, "I can't do this anymore. You deserve someone who can be with you for the rest of your life, someone who really loves you."

John threw himself on the ground and began to sob. I stared at him, feeling horrible inside. *I really am everything my mother told me I was,* I thought sadly. *I'm a bad person, a black widow. I've broken this poor guy's heart.*

John moved out. Not long after, my mother called, surprisingly chipper on the other line.

"Go look outside," she said cheerily.

I wandered over to the window, expecting to see her standing outside. Instead, I saw my car missing from the carport below. "My car's gone!" I cried, horrified.

"Yes. I have it, and you won't be getting it back anytime soon. You can't pay for it, so we're just going to take it."

You're kidding me! I sank to the ground, seething with anger. My father had helped cosign on the car for me, and I made payments through him. In his devastation, John had gone to my mother, and she had conspired to take my car away as a form of control and punishment for what I'd done. *You did it again, Mom. Anything to hurt me. How could you?*

Unable to get to work, I lost my job at the telemarketing place where I'd been employed. John's father came and removed all the furniture from our place, leaving me in an empty apartment all alone. With no money, job, food or car, I wondered what I'd do next. When the electricity got cut off, I huddled on the ground in the cold apartment, shivering without even a blanket.

And then I did something I had not done in a while. I prayed.

"God, I know you are not going to hear me because I've done so much bad stuff, but I'm going to try, anyway." I cried out to him, pleading for his help and direction. As I prayed, I drifted off to sleep.

I walked to the store the next morning, and when I returned, there was a lockbox fastened on the front door. *I officially have nowhere to go.*

I called a friend for help. "Do you have any money for a hotel?" I asked, desperate.

"No, but you can sleep in my car in my driveway if you want," my friend replied.

I decided to call my parents. "I have nowhere to go," I cried to my father when he answered. "Can I come back?"

"You're gonna have to talk to your mother," he replied.

I detected the submissiveness in my father's tone. With the tables now turned, my mother called all the shots, and my father did whatever she said.

My mother refused to let me come home, and I resorted to sleeping in my friend's car. *This is a new low,* I thought miserably as I tried to make myself comfortable that night. *I've officially hit a new low.*

I begged my grandmother to let me move in with her, and she relented. When she went to bed at 7 p.m. each night, I snuck out through the window and went out with friends. One night, at a car show in Sacramento, I met a guy named Jay. We eventually grew close. After my grandmother's curfew proved too strict for me to follow, I moved in with my cousin. But we had a falling out, and Jay asked me to move in with him.

"As friends," he promised. "We can share the expenses."

I landed a job at a bank and bunked up with Jay. I enjoyed our friendship and wondered if we could take our relationship further. We slept together, but I convinced myself I was not ready to fall in love. *I can't give my heart away again. I've already done that, and it proved too painful.*

One day, my stomach hurt more than usual, and I went to the doctor to have my ulcer checked out. The doctor returned with some news that shocked me.

"You're pregnant."

"I can't be," I stammered. I'd been told years before by a doctor that I might never conceive. How could this be happening?

Terror filled me. Due to the way I'd been raised, I'd decided I never wanted kids. But I also knew abortion was not an option. I believed in life and knew God did, also. Though I'd done many things I was ashamed of, I also still longed to please him deep down. I could not disappoint him or myself. I would go through with the pregnancy.

"This is great news!" Jay said excitedly when I told him.

My parents and his celebrated as well. But I did not. *Please, God, don't let it be a girl,* I prayed. I did not want a painful relationship like I'd endured with my mother. But then I remembered a necklace I'd once seen on a girl years before, bearing her name. *Renee. What a beautiful name,* I'd thought at the time. *Okay, God, if it is a little girl for some reason, her name will be Renee.*

One day, I decided it was time to get back in church. I had avoided it for years, not wanting to be like some of the phony Christians I'd seen growing up. But I knew I needed something good in my life, especially with a baby on the way. I picked up the phonebook and randomly selected a church. *North Bay Faith Center. That sounds nice.* I went by myself the following Sunday and sat in the back. I liked the pastor and what he had to say. *It feels good to be back in church. I need this right now.*

As the months went by and my belly swelled, my apprehension turned to excitement. I gave birth to a beautiful little girl and named her Renee. Immediately, I grew protective of her, wanting to shield her from the world. *I never knew I could love a little human being like this,* I thought, my heart warming as her soft skin touched mine.

When Renee was 9 months old, Jay and I got married. Though I was not in love with Jay, he was the sweetest guy I knew, and I was thrilled to have such a wonderful father for our daughter. Soon after, he began working 10- to 12-hour graveyard shifts. But our life was far from the newlywed fairytale. Jay and I rarely saw each other, and I often felt like a single mother. Money grew tighter than ever, and I wondered how I'd pay our bills.

Just when it seemed things couldn't get any worse, I

discovered I was pregnant again. I'd been on birth control, and the news came as a shock. Our family grew excited at the news, but I remained indifferent. *We can hardly pay the bills now. How are we going to feed one more mouth?* I thought worriedly.

Little David entered the world, a beautiful, perfect little boy. But immediately after, I plunged into postpartum depression. As the baby cried in the other room, I cried, too, not wanting to hold or feed him. Leaving the house felt like a major ordeal. Jay cared for the children until I was able to get better.

Money remained a constant struggle. We often scrambled to come up with the rent money and sometimes fell behind. But our wonderful apartment managers, Kay and Leon, took a liking to us and tried to help in whatever way they could. I was grateful for their kindness, though also a bit baffled. *Why are these people so nice to us? We've done nothing for them. In fact, they should have kicked us out by now.*

Jay began going to church with me at North Bay Faith Center, now renamed Celebration Church. Pastor Vernon had taken over, and I liked him a lot. We went from attending occasionally to going regularly. Everyone greeted us warmly, and like Kay and Leon's kindness, it surprised me. Growing up surrounded by chaos and fighting, I was not accustomed to people being so nice. *If only they really knew me,* I thought to myself. *If only they knew who I was and what I'd done. I wonder what they would think of me then.*

I brought David into church with me, and Renee attended a children's class. An elderly woman named Trudy sat behind me and reached out one Sunday.

"Let me have that baby," she said kindly as David began to cry.

I handed him over to her and watched in awe as she quietly soothed him. "It's okay. He's a good boy. A very good boy," she said sweetly.

Her gentle gesture impressed me. *There's such overwhelming love at this church! I've never seen anything like this before!*

As David's 1st birthday approached, Jay and I planned his party. Money was tight as usual, but my mother agreed to bring the food. We invited many of our new friends from church, and to my surprise, they all came. I glanced around nervously, wondering where my parents were. *They've got the food. If they don't show up soon, this party is going to be a huge flop,* I thought, growing panicked. As the minutes ticked by, my anxiety worsened, and I began to cry.

"What's wrong?" Pastor Vernon asked as he saw my tears.

Embarrassed, I explained the situation.

"Don't worry. We'll be right back."

Pastor Vernon left with another member of the church, and they returned with arms full of food and drinks. I watched in disbelief as they set everything up on the tables.

Who does this? I thought in awe, my heart deeply

touched by their generosity. *These people hardly know me, yet they've gone above and beyond for me.*

My parents arrived an hour later. I tried to rein in my anger. Once again, my past came back to haunt me — the tears, the fights, the name calling, the many nights I'd spent rocking myself to sleep in the corner of my room. *This won't last,* I thought sadly, glancing around at all the people from church. *They seem nice, but if they really knew me, they'd want nothing to do with me.*

Finances continued to be a struggle. It seemed there was never enough to pay the bills and barely enough to put food on the table. Though the children were too young for me to work, I tried pawning a few of my belongings to make a little cash. Jay and I began to fight frequently. His mother took a disliking to me as well, which only added to the stress in our marriage. I trudged through the days, trying to put on a brave face for the children but wondering how I'd survive.

One day, Jay went to the grocery store to get a money order to pay our $1,000 rent. He returned home with a pale face. "Don't be mad at me. I got the money order and put it in my pocket, but I forgot to sign it, and then somehow … I lost it."

I took a deep breath. Since attending church regularly, I had tried really hard to do the right thing, as difficult as it often was. Though I was tempted to blow up at Jay, I kept my cool. *Okay, God,* I prayed. *I am not going to fly off the handle here. Someone else must have needed that money more than us. We'll be okay somehow.*

The next day, we went to church. A woman approached me with an envelope. "God told me to give this to you," she said with a kind smile.

"Oh, thanks."

I stuck the envelope in my Bible, went home and forgot about it. Later that night as I was stressing about money, I felt a strong sense of urgency to check my Bible and the envelope I placed in there earlier that day. To my shock, $1,000 cash floated out. I nearly lost my balance. *Thank you, God! Oh, my goodness! You are so good to us!*

God continued to provide in amazing ways. When Pastor Vernon learned our electricity was about to be shut off, he gave us just enough money to keep the lights on. Other times, I went to the mailbox to find money for food inside. My heart swelled with appreciation at the generosity of near strangers. *I've done nothing for these people, yet they keep on loving on me. This is simply amazing!*

Jay and I continued to fight, and I eventually asked him to move out. He went to live with his mother and continued to see the children regularly. Now separated, I wondered how I'd get by. My heart sank as I reflected on our short-lived marriage. *Another guy who let me down. This seems to be the story of my life. Will I ever find true love? Or does it even exist?*

Christmas approached, and I had nothing for the kids. Desperate, I visited Dixon Family Services and asked if they could help.

"I'm sorry," the woman said. "But we have a policy to

offer one-time help, and you've already been here before."
Her eyes met mine, and she looked genuinely
disappointed that she could not help.

Rent was due again, and I knew I could not pay it. I
went down to the manager's office to talk to Kay. "I know
we owe you so much money," I told her with regret, trying
to hold back tears. "If you have to let us go, I completely
understand."

"Hey, you sell Mary Kay, don't you?" Kay asked.

I nodded. I had dabbled with the business for a while,
trying to earn a few extra bucks.

"Let me see what you have," she said.

I returned with the remains of my supply, and she
sifted through it. At last, she selected two lipsticks, an
eyeliner and a face cream. "Here, I'll give you $450 for
this," she said.

I gulped hard. *Four hundred and fifty dollars? Did I
hear her right?* "I don't know what to say ..." I stammered,
blown away by her gesture.

"Consider it a done deal." Kay smiled.

When rent came due the following month, I scrambled
once again. One night, after putting the kids to bed, I
stumbled into the living room and threw myself onto the
ground. "God, this isn't fair!" I cried. "I am trying my
hardest, and I don't know what to do. I have two kids, no
food and I don't want to be with Jay, but I don't know
what else to do."

And then I made a very big demand. "If you are the
God who everyone says you are, you have to show me that

you are real. I don't care about all the stuff I've heard through pastors and everyone else. I can't do this on my own. I need you to show me that you are real!"

In that moment, I wanted to die. But the thought of my two precious children kept me alive. As I finally drifted off to sleep that night, I prayed that things would change. I needed to escape this vicious cycle of hopelessness and defeat. I needed a miracle.

The next day, I went back down to Kay's office, my legs feeling like lead as I approached her with news that I could not pay rent again. I had decided to voluntarily evict myself this time. After a long conversation with Kay, we parted ways. To my surprise, a few hours later, she called me back down to her office.

Kay handed me a contract.

"What's this?" I asked, raising my brow.

"Look, Leon and I love you guys, and we can't imagine you being alone out there with those kids. We are going to take care of you. You sign this, saying you are going to stay in the apartment for $60 a month, and since I know you can't afford that, we'll eat the cost, and you'll stay here for free until you can get on your feet. Okay?"

I stared at her, incredulous. *Who does this sort of stuff? This is crazy!* Tears filled my eyes. Kay and Leon had become like family to me, closer than blood relatives. These Harley Davidson-loving, good-natured bikers did not care who I was. They simply cared about me, just as the church people did. The idea was astounding and almost too good to be true.

STRUCK

My hands trembled as I signed the contract. *God, you are so good. You sent these wonderful people to me in my time of need. You are real! Thank you!*

Knowing I needed to find a job, I went to an employment agency and learned a receptionist position at a doctor's office was immediately available. I obtained an interview with Dr. Edward. The minute the man walked into the room, I felt my face go hot. *Oh, my goodness, that is the most gorgeous man I've ever seen.* I was not easily attracted to men and had yet to find my Prince Charming, but I could hardly take my eyes off this man. As he fired off questions, I struggled to pay attention, too struck by his good looks.

"Do you speak Spanish?" Dr. Edward asked.

"Yes," I blurted. Though I didn't, I understood the language well. *If it gets me the job, so be it. I'm sure I can figure it out.*

Dr. Edward thanked me for coming in, and I left. I knew many people had applied for the job and didn't know if I stood a chance, especially having been out of the working world for a while. But one thing was certain — I could not get his face out of my head.

One day, I opened the door to find my friend Sally standing there with a giant Christmas tree and some food. "I figured you'd need this," she said with a sheepish smile.

I stared at her, my face breaking into a smile. I knew Sally struggled financially herself, but she had found it in her heart to deliver a beautiful act of kindness just days before Christmas. The kids' eyes widened with delight as they saw the tree, and my heart warmed. "You, tiny little thing, dragged that heavy tree all the way up those steps?" I teased Sally. "Thank you. I don't know what else to say."

A few weeks later, someone knocked on the door again. It was the woman from Dixon Family Services, bearing a wagon full of gifts. "The organization can't help you, but I can," she said. "I saw your face when you came into the office, and I just had to help."

Oh, God, thank you. Again, tears filled my eyes. I'd asked God to show me that he was real, and he had gone above and beyond to demonstrate his love and care.

Just when it seemed the miracles could not get any better, I got a phone call. It was Dr. Edward's office, offering me the job. *God, you are too good! You continue to show me personally that you care about me. You are providing in amazing ways.*

As I began working with Dr. Edward, I became drawn not just to his good looks but his generosity and compassion as well. He often gave his patients rides and even bought an elderly man a pair of shoes. *This guy has to be a Christian,* I decided. *Who else would do something like that?*

I learned Dr. Edward had a girlfriend. Since I was still technically married to Jay, I knew it was wrong to pursue a relationship, especially with my boss. But I was drawn to Dr. Edward like a magnet, and I could not resist. One day, I worked up the courage to ask him to coffee.

"Sorry, but I have to pick up my son," Dr. Edward replied regretfully.

Oh, he has a son. I see. The walls I'd started to tear down quickly went back up. Dr. Edward then began to pursue me, but I resisted his advances. I went to the women's meetings at church and asked the women to help me pray him out of my life.

"How do you know it's God's will for you to pray him out of your life?" a woman asked.

"I just do. There's no way it could work," I replied.

I learned Dr. Edward had grown up as a Buddhist, not a Christian. *Well, there goes that,* I decided. *One more reason not to date him.*

One day, a patient came into the office. "You like Dr. Edward, don't you?" he asked, smiling.

I blushed. "What? Well, it doesn't matter. He's not a Christian," I replied quickly.

"Not now, but he will be," the man replied with a twinkle in his eye.

And then, to my surprise, he laid his hand on my head and began praying for me. "Lord, help her with her children," he began.

How does he know I have children? This is crazy!

I learned the man was a pastor from Oakland. I was blown away at his words. *What are you up to, God? Are you trying to tell me something?*

Dr. Edward asked me out to coffee again, and this time, I agreed. "We're actually having an Easter play at our church this Sunday. You're welcome to come, and we could go out afterward," I suggested, knowing full well he probably wouldn't show up.

But to my surprise, the following Sunday, Dr. Edward walked in just as the church service started and planted himself in the first row. After the service, Pastor Vernon asked if anyone wanted to accept Jesus as his or her Savior. To my shock, Dr. Edward stepped forward to pray.

"I may have grown up Buddhist, but I always knew there was more out there," he told me. "Today, I found that out."

Oh, God, you are so good! Another miracle!

Dr. Edward and I began hanging out regularly. One night, we slept together. Not long after, I learned I was pregnant. *How could this be? We were only together one time!* Shame filled me. *God, this is not okay. What am I going to do?* I began to freak out.

I shared with my mother that I was thinking about terminating the pregnancy. I wanted her to talk me out of it, but seemingly without emotion, she asked me, "When are you going to do it?" In the following days, my mother pressed me about my decision to see if I had gone through with it. I also confided in Pastor Vernon and his wife, who encouraged me to keep the baby. But I didn't see how I could.

If I tell Edward, he'll surely run. I can't be a single mother of three kids. There's only one thing left to do. I need to keep this secret to myself and have an abortion. I know it's wrong, but there are no other options. If I go through with this pregnancy, my life could be ruined.

I made an appointment for the procedure and learned I needed someone to drive me home. *Who am I gonna call?* Desperate, I dialed Jay's number, knowing he would be furious when he learned the news.

"Are you kidding me, Vivian?" he cried. "Not only have you cheated on me, but you are pregnant, and you want *me* to take you to get an abortion! You are such a b****!"

I had never heard him call me such a name before. But I knew I deserved it. I had done a terrible thing.

In all of his anger and pain, he knew I had no one else. Jay set aside his own feelings and drove me to the doctor's office, and I underwent the horrible procedure. After going home, the pain intensified, and I writhed on the bathroom floor and cried. *How am I in this place when I was just trying to get my act together? I can only imagine the way Jay must feel over what I've done! I am a mess!*

Jay drove me back to the doctor's, where I screamed in pain as the nurses came in. *Oh, God, I am so sorry. There is no worse person than me right now. How did I let this happen? You've done so much for me, and I've spit in your face. This is what I do. I hurt people.*

I kept my terrible secret from Edward, and he continued to pursue me. One day, he informed me that he needed to let me go. "If we're going to see each other, you can't work here. But don't worry. I'm going to take care of you, Vivian." He then asked me to meet his son.

"Look, I don't have anything," I told him. "I don't know what you think you are going to get being with me."

But Edward persisted. Knowing my car had been repossessed, he took me down to a dealership and paid cash for a new car for me. "I can't leave you with two kids and no car," he said. "You don't understand. This is so not me, doing something like this. But I just feel that I have to."

Again, I shook my head in disbelief. *Who is this man, and what have I done to deserve his goodness?* I thought of the abortion. If he only knew.

At the height of my pain, Kay and Leon informed me that they were moving away.

"Please take me with you," I begged them through my tears. They had become like family to me, and I could not imagine life without them.

The day they drove away, I stood in the driveway and let the tears fall in a flood. *There goes the best thing that ever happened to me. What will I do now?*

My apartment complex went downhill, and crime worsened. Edward asked me to move in with him, and though I wanted to take that next step with him, I felt he was taking pity on me. I wanted it for the right reasons, but I was scared of his intentions. Crime got really bad, and it became so unsafe. Edward insisted I move in with him. He had just purchased a large five-bedroom house with plenty of room. I agreed to move in with him.

I moved in with Edward, but I took a step back from the church. I knew I'd made some mistakes and was filled with shame and regret. Pastor Vernon continued to leave encouraging messages on my voicemail, and I appreciated his gesture. *That man never gives up on me. What love and compassion.*

STRUCK

One day, while driving, I joked about being married, like I did many times before. This time it seemed as if Edward wasn't playing anymore. He took me to a jewelry store, and we looked for a bit, all the while with me still thinking that he was being playful. To my shock, he bought the ring! I left the store still in astonishment. In the car, Edward asked me to be his wife.

As I stared into his beautiful face, I realized I had loved him all along. "Yes," I whispered. "I will."

Edward and I went to counseling at the cathedral where we planned to marry. Meanwhile, we abstained from intimacy and slept in separate bedrooms, which was especially difficult. But after making several mistakes, I wanted to honor God. Deep down, I was terrified at giving marriage another chance. *I want to do things right this time, God. I don't want to mess it up.*

Edward and I married, and I learned right away I was pregnant. Nine months after we walked down the aisle, we welcomed a little boy into the world. I marveled at my three beautiful gifts and the treasure I gained through marriage, my new son, Isaiah. *I was once told I'd never have children, then convinced myself I didn't want them and now look how God has blessed me! Despite all I've done, he is so faithful and good.*

Edward offered me a lifestyle I'd never imagined in my wildest dreams. My days of poverty were long gone, replaced by a large home, several cars and plenty of money in the bank. I'd gone from sleeping in cars, getting my electricity shut off and struggling to put food on the table to having more than enough. When I'd been down and out, I'd once vowed that I would find a way to help people when my life improved. Now, I'd finally be able to do that. It was time to pay it forward.

As anyone knows, money does not buy happiness. Edward and I struggled to blend our families together, both having different ideas on parenting. We began to fight often. We returned to Celebration Church and asked Pastor Vernon to counsel us.

"I don't think I can do this anymore," I admitted to Pastor Vernon, my eyes welling with tears. "I think it's over."

Edward nodded in his seat. "I'm not sure I can live with her, either," he said sadly.

Pastor Vernon prayed with us and encouraged us to make things work. We plugged ourselves back into church, and our friends embraced us as though we'd never even left.

There is no place I'd rather be, I decided. *This is definitely my home and my family. This is where we belong.*

The more Christ became the center of our home, the more our family thrived. Edward and I began getting along, and the kids began to thrive. They each developed a love for God, and I thanked God for working in their little hearts. Slowly, the wall I'd worked so hard to build came crumbling down, as I learned to accept my husband's love, as well as God's. *I may have come from a hurting place, but I do not have to repeat what I experienced in my home growing up. God has given me a fresh start, and I will embrace it to the fullest.*

Four years after we married, I discovered a lump in my breast. Immediately, I knew something was wrong. Breast cancer ran in my family, and I was certain the lump was cancerous.

Edward and I prayed together but told no one except Pastor Vernon. On the day of my biopsy, I walked into the doctor's office, completely terrified. To my surprise, I saw Pastor Vernon standing there with his mother. Relief overwhelmed me. *Oh, what love this man has! He has come to support me in my darkest hour.*

Pastor Vernon prayed with us in the lobby while the nurses watched from nearby. The nurse then called me in and allowed Edward to come as well. She asked me which side the lump was on, and I told her. After a long while of searching the previous mammograms, she turned to me, completely confused. "I'm going to have to go get the doctor, because I can't find the lump," she said.

I burst into tears. "Praise God!" I cried. At that very moment, I knew I'd been healed.

The doctor came in and began searching, but he was boggled as well. "I'm not quite sure what happened, but that lump is no longer there," he confirmed.

I continued to praise God, and the doctor seemed irritated.

"Was the lump there this morning?" he asked.

I nodded.

He became more determined, but after finding

nothing, he suggested I return in three months for a recheck.

You don't know my God, mister, because my God heals, and when he does, he heals for good! Praise him!

Edward and I rejoiced at the miracle. God's kindness continued to abound in ways we could not understand. But his work was not over yet.

ॐॐॐ

Ten years after Kay and Leon moved away, I reconnected with them on Facebook. Kay, thrilled to speak to me after so long, let me know that Leon was very sick. God pressed it on my heart to go visit him right away. I sped to the hospital, praying all the way that it would not be too late when I arrived. Leon had played such a special part in my life, and I'd never be able to thank him enough for all he'd done for me.

Kay and I reunited in the hospital halls, screaming and crying as we embraced. I'd never been happier to see someone in all my life. She led me in to see Leon, who was barely recognizable in his pale, feeble state. I squeezed his hand, and to my surprise, he moved.

"He hasn't moved at all in four days," Kay gasped.

"Leon, you took care of me when I had nobody else. I believe God is going to take care of you," I whispered through my tears.

Leon's eyes opened, and he squeezed my hand again and tried to speak. His family watched our interaction with awe. I went home, praying, confident that God would heal Leon. But when the phone rang the next day, I learned devastating news. Leon had passed away.

For the first time in my life, I grew angry with God. *How could you let him die, God? You promised me he would be okay!*

Concerned, Edward called Pastor Vernon, who encouraged me to get back to church. I went, but though I was present physically, I was not present emotionally. I could not stop thinking of Leon. I wasn't sure if he had accepted Christ before he'd died, and I wanted to see him in heaven someday.

"How do you know he was not saved?" Pastor Vernon asked me. "You never know what God can do."

Pastor Vernon then shared a story with me from his wife. "At the earlier Sunday service, God spoke to Tina. He told her these words: 'Don't worry, my child, he is with me.' But strangely, I felt like those words were meant for someone not sitting in that service. Now, I know they were meant for you. Leon is in heaven with Jesus."

"Oh, thank you!" I cried. I rejoiced, knowing I could rest in peace at last. Though I would miss Leon terribly, I was thankful he would spend eternity with Jesus.

Kay's family asked me to perform the funeral, and I grew terrified. How could I do such a thing? But I loved her like blood, and I knew I had to do it as a gesture of love. After all, they'd done so much for me.

I picked out the songs and decided to make a CD for every guest. When I arrived at the ceremony, I spotted dozens of Harley Davidson motorcycles outside. "How am I supposed to go in there and do this?" I asked Edward, shaking.

But the moment I took the stage, God completely overwhelmed me with his peace. He began to speak through me, and as I spoke, people dabbed at their eyes and cried. A man came up to me afterward with some amazing words.

"Years ago, Kay and Leon had really gone through some tough stuff. They asked me to help them, and I did. But I told them they needed to help others someday. After hearing your story, it's sure obvious they did. You are gonna do the same thing someday, and God will bless you for it."

Oh, thank you, God, for these words! What an encouragement to know their story has come full circle! I fully intend to pay it forward.

Kay's sister approached me, too. "Kay and her children accepted Jesus into their lives years ago, but Leon was the only one who hadn't. That is, until you prayed for him. Now the family is complete. I cannot thank you enough."

Again, I rejoiced. I thought back to the day Kay had sat with me in her office, picking through my Mary Kay items. Her generosity had always astounded me. Now I understood why she'd been so kind. She loved Jesus, and because of him, she showered that love on me. In a world of people who often claimed to be Christians but acted differently, Kay was the real deal. I would never forget her or Leon as long as I lived.

After the funeral, strangers began to contact me on Facebook, letting me know that they'd invited Christ into their hearts after listening to the CDs I'd made. I thanked God for using me in ways I'd never imagined.

Oh, God, I prayed as I read their heartfelt messages, *you have given me more than I deserve. You've taken a broken, hurting girl and restored my heart. You've provided for me in miraculous ways, even when life seemed impossible. You've blessed me with an amazing church full of people who love you, as well as a pastor who represents you like no one I've ever met. You've given me a husband who treats me like a queen, as well as four beautiful children who love you. I could not ask for more.*

I thought back to the night I'd thrown myself on the floor in tears in my little apartment, convinced I'd come to the end of myself. I'd wanted to die that night. The years of abuse, hurtful words, broken relationships, financial struggles and bad decisions had all come to a head, and I'd been without hope. But God had intervened, and he had shown himself real. He had taught me that even when people failed, I could trust him. Even when I'd done shameful, wrong things, he had not given up on me. He pursued me with his unrelenting love, never giving up. And in the end, that love won me over.

Life's hardships may continue, but I will face them with strength and persevere. I have all I need — I have Jesus. And his love never fails.

SECOND CHANCES
THE STORY OF BETHANY
WRITTEN BY KAREN KOCZWARA

"Something is not right!" I shouted to the doctors, sudden panic racing through me.

Moments later, the heart monitor began beeping wildly, and the hospital staff jumped into action, checking my vitals, along with the baby's.

We've got trouble!

Heart rate's off the chart!

We gotta act fast!

Gonna lose the baby.

Can only save one of them!

I lay helpless on the cold operating table as the doctor and nurses rushed to my side, prepping for emergency surgery.

"Save the baby!" I cried, unable to bear the thought of losing my child.

"Save my wife!" my husband interjected, his face pale and stricken with fear as he stood nearby.

"No, save the baby!" I argued.

How is this happening again?

My mind snapped back to the first nightmare nearly 10 years before. Another hospital bed. Another terrible scare. Two lives on the line. And an angel with a message, telling me my time was not up. *Is this it? Is my time up now? Is it too late to save both our lives?*

❧ ❧ ❧

I was born near Fort Lauderdale, Florida, in 1960, the second youngest of 10 children. My father, a war veteran, turned to alcohol and was unable to hold a job. My mother worked hard as a nurse and later found work as a manager at a plastic company. She tried her hand at bingo to drum up extra cash, but there never seemed to be enough to go around, and we grew accustomed to being poor. We moved frequently, hopping between houses and apartments in search of cheaper rent. As my father's drinking increased, his health grew worse. My siblings and I tiptoed around him when he was drunk, not wanting to upset him. He eventually lost his eyesight. Life became a constant struggle of ups and downs, and I learned from an early age to fight for my place in the world.

When I was 7, I began smoking pot with my older brothers and sisters. There always seemed to be a pipe lying around the house, and I figured the habit was harmless. I enjoyed school until the sixth grade, and then I grew restless. At 14, I signed up for work experience at school and landed a job at the local Burger King. The job provided a few extra bucks of spending money and a chance to escape the chaos in our house. That same year, I took up drinking. It offered another temporary escape. *I'm going to do what I want from now on,* I decided.

SECOND CHANCES

At 15, I moved to Virginia to be near my sister. She took me to church with her a few times, and I enjoyed the services. I'd ridden the bus to the local Baptist church a few times as a kid and always enjoyed Sunday school. Now, sitting there in the pews, many of the Bible stories came back to me. As the pastor spoke about God and read from the Bible, I listened attentively. *Could there really be a God out there who cares about me?* I thought of my alcoholic father, traumatized by the war, unable to work, a slave to the bottle. I thought of my mother, working so hard to provide for 10 children and keeping us from plummeting into poverty. *Is God really good?*

While in Virginia, I met a guy, and we began dating. Not long after, I learned I was pregnant. Scared and uncertain what to do, I confided in my mother.

"You're going to be okay, Bethany," she assured me. "I will be there for you, and we'll get through this."

I told my boyfriend about the pregnancy, and he promised to be there for me. I decided to go through with the pregnancy, watching as my belly swelled and grew bigger each month. As my due date approached, I grew more anxious. At 15, I still had much to learn about life and parenting. But I had also seen more hardship than many would in a lifetime, and growing up with such a large family had prepared me to assert my independence. I would find a way to make a life for my child and myself.

Shortly before my due date, I awoke with a horrible side-splitting pain. The doctor had described the birth pains I might feel, but this seemed abnormal. *I don't think this pain is where it's supposed to be,* I thought with alarm. When it worsened to an unbearable level, I called my doctor, and he admitted me to the hospital two towns over to deliver the baby.

The nurses settled me in, and I writhed on the bed, the pain escalating with every passing moment. As I drifted in and out of consciousness, the sterile hospital room became a blur. Whirring machines, bright lights and doctors' voices floated around me as I groggily opened and closed my eyes. As the pain pressed in, I wondered how much more I could bear.

"Everything is going to be okay," the nurse said calmly, trying to comfort me.

"Who is having this baby? Me or you?" I snapped.

A doctor showed up on emergency call. He had just been reading up on the complications of toxemia and was concerned about my condition. After transferring me to the Intensive Care Unit, he began running some tests. When my blood work came back, he grew gravely concerned. "Her blood pressure has shot up, and her platelets have dropped. We have to get this girl into emergency surgery right now!" he ordered.

The doctors wheeled me down the hall, shouting orders to each other as they ran.

"If we don't operate right away, she's not gonna make it!"

Too dazed to respond, I lay back on the bed, my head pounding, my heart racing as the baby and I both fought for our lives. And then a very strange thing happened.

Suddenly, I felt that I was floating, looking down on the operating room below from a rooftop corner. I saw the mirrors and the backs of the doctors' heads as they frantically sprang into action. My view then shifted, and I found myself floating above the waiting room, watching as the clergyman somberly spoke to my worried mother.

"I'm here! I'm right here!" I tried to call out, but no one noticed me.

The next thing I knew, I saw a very bright light and, with it, what appeared to be … an angel? Though her facial features were vague, she looked slightly familiar. *Is she an old friend? Do I know her somehow?* "It is not your time," she told me gently, her smile comforting and kind. "You need to go back to earth now."

But I did not want to go back. In an instant, I felt completely warm, content and at ease. Wherever I was, I liked it. For a moment, all of my worries faded away in the midst of the bright light. *I could stay here forever,* I thought happily.

I awoke in a hospital bed, my eyesight blurry, my head still pounding. The crisp sheets felt cold against my skin, and the same familiar buzzing and bleeping of the machines sounded in the background. Somewhere far off, I heard a doctor's voice. I wiggled my fingers and toes, trying to convince myself I was not dreaming. *I am alive. I am back on earth. What was that all about? How long have I been gone?*

And then I remembered the baby. *My baby! I need to see my baby!*

"We thought we lost you." A doctor appeared at my side, and I tried to make out the blurry features of his face. "How are you doing, Bethany?"

"Okay. How is … how is my baby?"

"You have a beautiful, healthy little girl. Full term, great weight. Came out with long fingernails and everything. You can see her when you are well."

A little girl! My heart surged with happiness. *At least the baby is safe. She is going to be okay.*

My mother arrived next, her face etched with relief. "Oh, honey, we thought we lost you. Everyone was so concerned. A clergyman came and told us to prepare for the worst. You were drifting in and out of consciousness, and your blood pressure soared so high they could not get it under control. The doctors had to perform an emergency C-section and cut you straight down the belly. Do you remember talking to me when you were in between consciousness? You were murmuring, describing the room and what the doctors were doing."

I tried to think hard. Bits and pieces of the ordeal were returning to me. "I think so," I replied quietly. I recalled the bright light, the angel and the message she'd delivered. *It's not your time yet.* She must have been a messenger from God, sent straight from heaven! Had I been floating between heaven and earth in some sort of supernatural realm?

When I held my daughter for the very first time, she was even more beautiful than the doctor had described. Joy overwhelmed me as I surveyed her plump pink skin, tiny features and long fingernails. *You are safe in my arms, little baby. We will figure out this world together. We've made it this far already.*

I went back to live with my mother and spent my days caring for the baby. My boyfriend proved unpredictable, unable to hold down a job. Concerned about money, I took up two part-time jobs to provide for my daughter. But on top of caring for an infant, the work became wearisome.

I came home one day to discover that my boyfriend had left and was nowhere to be seen. My mother, sympathetic as usual, told me to quit one of my jobs.

"You can't keep working two jobs, honey. It's going to take a toll on you. I'll help you care for the baby. You'll be okay."

My boyfriend returned out of the blue a month later and announced he had joined up with some sort of mafia group. We parted ways, and I decided I didn't care if I ever saw him again. We were both young and had our whole lives ahead of us. I would find a way to raise my daughter on my own.

My days became a blur of housework, laundry, work and diaper changing. I met another guy at work. Slim, at 5 feet, 6 inches and 150 pounds, he seemed handsome and sweet. We began dating, and after a year, we decided to get married. He agreed to adopt my daughter as his own, and I was grateful for the gesture. I hoped that his salary might be able to relieve some of the financial pressure I faced. But within no time, his jealous side appeared. If another guy even so much as walked in front of me, he grew furious.

"I saw you flirting with that guy," he accused me. "You were totally making eyes at him."

"What are you talking about?" I shot back. "I wasn't doing any such thing."

Our conflict only worsened, and we decided to divorce. I continued working, but shared custody of my daughter with my ex-husband. I met a new guy, and he seemed to take a genuine interest in me. "I'm moving out to California," he announced one day. "You should come out, too."

Eager for a change of pace and some fresh scenery, I decided to take him up on the offer. My ex-husband offered to keep my daughter with him until I got settled, and I agreed. I followed my new boyfriend across the country, hopeful for the new adventures that awaited.

We arrived in Northern California, settling near the Bay Area. But almost immediately, my boyfriend ran off with his boss' daughter. A month later, he married her, leaving me behind in the dust. I was now stuck in a new town without any friends and not a clue how to get home.

I located an uncle nearby and stayed with him until I could get on my feet.

"Don't worry. You can stay as long as you need to," he assured me.

I found work as a bartender at a local bar. Regular patrons wandered in to play cards, have a few rounds, smoke and socialize. I hung out with them, drinking, partying and smoking pot every night. The dim lights, clanging glasses, blaring background music and constant chatter comprised my new home away from home. As I learned the patrons' names and learned their stories, they became like a second family to me. When closing time arrived, I wiped the counters clean and headed home with the fistful of tips that would hopefully pay my bills.

A year and a half after moving to California, I met a guy named Mike. At 6 feet, 2 inches and 260 pounds, with broad shoulders and a full beard, Mike looked like the typical biker that would intimidate any guy in a bar. But beneath his tough exterior was a sweet, irresistible personality. Mike seemed to know everyone in town, and when he walked into the bar, everyone high-fived him and called out his name. We began dating and married, and shortly after we wed, I discovered I was pregnant.

As my due date neared, my doctors discussed my delivery. Because of the trauma surrounding my first birth, they advised a C-section. After admitting me to give birth, the anesthesiologist wheeled me into the operating room and administered a spinal block. But he did not back the needle out of the blood vessel all the way, and the anesthesia went straight to my heart. Within moments, I knew something was wrong. My heart began to race, and I felt lightheaded and dizzy.

"There's a problem," I told the doctors with urgency. "Something is wrong here."

Suddenly, the heart monitors began to jump all over the place, and the doctors sprang into action.

"She's right. Something is not right here. Her heart rate is going crazy."

The doctors gave me another shot, trying to counteract the spinal block with Novocain. I watched as their brows furrowed with concern, and fear overcame me. My mind snapped to my daughter's traumatic birth, when I'd momentarily died on the operating table. I thought of the bright light and the angel with the message: "It's not your time yet." *This is happening all over again. Oh, God, it's happening all over again. Is it my time now?*

"The baby or your wife … we can't save them both," the doctors told my husband. "You have to decide. Fast."

"The baby! Save the baby!" I cried, glancing down at my belly, where our child fought for his life inside.

"Save my wife," my husband interjected, shaking his head. "Save her."

"No, save the baby!" I protested. *This isn't really happening. I'm living a nightmare right now. Oh, God, I'm living a nightmare.*

"We're going to operate. We'll try to get the baby out and save them both."

The doctors cut me open, while I remained completely conscious and helpless on the other end of the curtain. The heart rate monitors continued to beep in alarm, and I tried to ignore them. My husband paced the floor nearby, waiting for the doctors' next words. And then, after what felt like the longest few minutes of our entire lives, we heard a wonderful, beautiful sound — a baby's cry. Our baby was alive!

SECOND CHANCES

"You have a healthy little boy," the doctor announced, placing my son near my chest. "Congratulations."

I breathed a huge sigh of relief, and my husband rushed to my side to take a peek at our tiny son.

"He's perfect," we whispered, examining his miniature features beneath the soft blanket. "Just perfect."

After stabilizing me, the doctors wheeled me back to recovery. The adrenaline drained from my veins as the anesthesia wore off, and I breathed a prayer of gratitude. *Wow, that was really close. But our son is alive and thriving, and that's what's most important. We're all going to be okay.*

Six months after my son's birth, I sent for my daughter. Now 10 years old, she had struggled to get along with my ex-husband's new wife, and she was happy to reunite with me. I introduced her to her baby brother, and she expressed excitement over her new sibling. For a moment, everything felt complete again. I had a new husband, a stable income, a home and two children I loved. But not everything in our lives was stable, and I'd soon be thrust back into chaos.

I continued bartending and hanging out with Mike's group of friends, which included a bunch of rough bikers. The Hell's Angels, a notorious motorcycle gang, approached him several times, wanting him to join. I had grown up around guys in the Hell's Angels and was accustomed to their fearless lifestyle. They knew better than to mess with me. We kept up our partying ways, staying out late after work, drinking and smoking pot with other folks at the bars. The cycle of drinking and drugs soon took its toll on our marriage. Our relationship grew tumultuous, and before long, we separated.

I kept my daughter with me, and Mike and I began fighting for custody of our young son. The battle grew ugly, as neither of us was willing to budge. At last, the courts stepped in.

"If you two cannot agree on an arrangement, we will have to take your son away from you and put him in temporary care until you can come up with a plan," they told us firmly.

"All right, look, Mike," I said with a sigh. "You hear what the courts are telling us. We need to work things out."

Mike relented, and we figured out a compromise. But my heart still broke for our failed relationship. As a young girl, I'd heard the hurtful words, "You will never amount to anything." I'd spent my whole life wanting to be loved, hoping I might find it in a relationship with a guy. *Perhaps this one will be it,* I'd told myself each time. And when things did not work out, I couldn't help but wonder, *What is wrong with me? Am I not loveable? Will anyone ever accept me just as I am? Am I meant to spend the rest of my life alone?*

I kept up bartending and tried to focus on the kids. Mike lost his job and spent his time dealing drugs to make a living. We both continued hanging around a rough group, including several Hell's Angels bikers. Though I brought in a decent amount of money from tips each night, it was not always enough to pay the bills. Things grew tighter and tighter, and I wondered how I'd be able to feed and clothe the kids, much less keep the electricity on.

I began hanging out with a guy named Chris, who dealt drugs as well. One night, a girl showed up at my house, furious. "Where are the drugs?" she demanded when I opened the door.

"What are you talking about?" I asked, confused.

"Chris didn't deliver. He was supposed to show up, and he didn't. So where are they?"

"Look, I don't know what you're talking about," I retorted. "I'm not involved in any of this. If you mess with me, I'll hunt you down, so don't you come knocking at my door."

The girl stormed away, fuming. I had a feeling this wasn't over.

When Chris showed up at my house the next day, I interrogated him. "Look, this girl came over saying you didn't deliver. You're not doing your job, man, and you're going to get us both in trouble."

"It's all good. Just calm down," he shot back.

One of the guys from the local club where I worked showed up a short time later. "Have you guys seen Carrie? No one has seen her since you threatened her last night, and now there's a story going around that you murdered her and she's lying on the side of the street somewhere."

Murdered? "That's crazy. I would never do such a thing," I snapped. "That's totally crazy."

By the end of the day, we learned some staggering news. Carrie had indeed been murdered, along with her boyfriend and another young man. The police were looking for Chris, certain he was involved somehow. And because I was the last one to see Carrie and had threatened her, they were looking for me, too.

Three young people dead. Three innocent lives robbed. Oh, God. Another living nightmare.

Before I could attempt to figure things out, the cops showed up at my door.

"Sit down, and shut up," they barked, slapping handcuffs on my wrists.

Frightened, I did as they said, watching in horror as they stormed through the house and raided it. I knew they were looking for evidence, perhaps a body stashed in a closet somewhere. *I didn't do it!* I wanted to scream. *I'm innocent!* But I knew my protests would do no good. The truth was, I'd been mixed up with the wrong crowd, and it had finally caught up with me. I'd have to save my rebuttals for court, when I could give my defense before a jury.

The cops arrested Chris and another guy named Richard. A series of exhausting trials stretched through the next year and a half. The details were gruesome. Carrie's face had been shot off. Her boyfriend had been shot twice, and the third young man's life had been taken when the perpetrators set him on fire in his car. There had been some dispute about a stolen car stereo. I cringed each time they laid out the horrific scene. I glanced over at Chris and

Richard, sitting stoically in their seats. *Did you do it, guys? Did you really do it? How could you? Don't you see how you've ruined all our lives, including mine?*

Meanwhile, I learned some other devastating news. My beloved mother had been diagnosed with cancer, and it was spreading fast. I needed to get back home and see her, but how could I in the midst of this mess? I prayed, asking God to please help me find a way to see her before it was too late.

God, please, you gotta do something so I can get back and see my mom. You just gotta help me, please. I had spoken to God on and off over the years, but I wasn't sure he still heard my prayers. It had been a long time since I'd set foot in church, and I knew I'd gotten far off track. Deep down, I wanted to believe that God loved me, that he hadn't given up on me. *But had I gone too far this time? Did he really care about the details of my screwed-up life?*

In his confession, Richard told the jury that I talked Chris into killing the girl. But after finding no evidence to back up these statements, the courts released me with charges still pending. I flew home to see my mother and learned the cancer had moved into her liver. Devastated, I sat with her, holding her hand and trying to soak up the precious time we had left together.

"I love you, Mom," I said, tears filling my eyes. "It's all going to be okay." I spoke to her, as well as to myself, trying to reassure myself that when I returned to California, the courts would find complete favor with me.

I said goodbye to my mother, knowing it might be the

last time I'd ever see her. And as I climbed onto the plane and headed back to the West Coast, I thanked God for giving me the opportunity to see her before she died. My mother had lived a difficult life, doing the best she could to raise 10 children while working to provide for us as well. She had helped me get back on my feet after the birth of my daughter, and I would always be grateful for that. *I'll find a way to make it all right, Mom, for both of us. I promise.*

I wrote several letters to Chris and sent them to the prison, but they all came back unanswered. He severed all ties with me, clearly not interested in associating with me anymore. A second trial ensued, and my nightmare continued. Police officers bugged my house and followed me everywhere. Many times, while driving, I glanced back to see their cars just a few feet behind me. *Just keep cool, Bethany. You know you didn't do it. You know you are innocent. Don't let them get to you.*

But their constant pursuit did get to me. "This has to stop," I told my defense lawyer wearily. "I can't even eat or sleep without feeling like I'm being followed. It's getting really old."

"I hear they're close to a verdict, and it's going to come out in your favor," my lawyer replied. "Just hang in there."

One day, while driving, I headed up a large hill and pulled into a parking lot. As I turned off the car, I began to pray. *God, I don't know what's going on. I don't know if Chris did it or not. I need your help. I'm scared, and I'm tired of living like this, always being followed. I know I've gotten mixed up with the wrong crowd, but I don't know what to do now. I don't know how to get out of this.* As I talked to him, the tears began to roll down my face, and I did not try to stop them. I was exhausted, at the end of myself and completely alone. I had two kids who needed me, a dying mother and a murder verdict on the line. Things had grown extremely complicated, and I hadn't a clue how to pull out of everything on my own. If there was any hope, it had to be in God. I was pretty sure he was the only one who could rescue me from this mess.

For the next two hours, I cried and poured my heart out to God. At last, I climbed out of the car and sat on the front hood. And then, as clearly as if he was sitting right next to me, I heard God say, "I will take care of you. You will be okay, Bethany."

Oh, God, really? I breathed a sigh of relief. *I am going to be okay. God has told me I will. I am going to trust in him.*

The police pulled into the parking lot a few minutes later. "I'm going to be okay. I'm going home now," I told them. I hopped back into the car and headed home, completely mentally and physically exhausted. But beyond the exhaustion, I felt something else I hadn't felt in a very long time — a small glimmer of hope. And with it, an ounce of peace.

I spent the next several days driving around, thinking about my life, waiting on edge as the trial came to a close. There would be a verdict soon, and I needed to be prepared for the worst. I had been charged with aiding and abetting a murder. Though I was a petite 5 feet, 1 inch, and the other guys on trial towered over me at 6 feet tall, they had tried to pin me as the ringleader in the murder. I only hoped the court would come to its senses and see that I was an innocent woman. I would then try to resume any normalcy I could.

One day, while driving aimlessly down the street, I thought to myself, *Where did I end up last time, anyway?* I turned and headed back up the same hill I'd gone up before, and to my amazement, I realized where I'd parked. It was a Christian church!

Wow, God, you spoke to me right here in the parking lot of a Christian church. Surely, that can't be coincidence. Surely, you meant what you said. You are going to take care of me, and I will be okay.

A month later, my mother passed away. I went back to Florida for her funeral and reunited with my brothers and sisters. We had all scattered in various directions, our once-tight-knit family now split apart. Though we'd endured poverty, alcoholism and plenty of scuffles growing up, we were still family at the end of the day. And family was what I needed most right now, at a time when I felt completely alone.

"Don't go back to California," my family told me when I updated them on the trial. "We'll hide you here."

"I have to go back, guys," I told them. "I have to listen to God."

While in Florida, the jury reached a verdict. They found Richard and Chris both guilty.

SECOND CHANCES

Richard was sentenced to life with the possibility of parole, while Chris was sentenced to life in prison without parole. Chris had made a foolish mistake when he asked the judge if he could talk to the jury. He'd said too much, and the verdict was not in his favor. Richard had confessed his part in assisting with the murder. My future still lay on the line, uncertain. But for now, I had some closure.

Just when it seemed things might settle down, I received a devastating call.

"Bethany? Mike and your son have been in a motorcycle accident. Your son is okay, but Mike is in bad shape."

"I'll be right there." I hung up, my heart pounding as I sped off to the hospital. *Oh, please, God, let them be okay. Please.* Though Mike and I had now been divorced for several years, we still remained good friends. I could not fathom the idea of anything happening to him.

I arrived at the hospital and learned Mike had lost his leg when he flew over the top of his motorcycle. I thanked God for protecting him and my son from further harm. But his struggles were just beginning. He now faced a lifetime of challenges with his new handicap.

Wanting to do something to help, I offered to move back in with Mike until he could get himself settled. I tended to his leg three times a day and took care of all the other household duties. "When you are able to move around, I'll get you settled on state disability and move out," I told him.

"Thanks, Bethany. You're a real lifesaver." Mike looked up at me gratefully. "This is really hard, but it would be even harder without you."

A short time later, the Hell's Angels put on a benefit to raise money for Mike. I decided to attend the event to support him. It would not be easy to face this tough crowd. I knew many of them still questioned whether or not I had anything to do with the murder. *I must face them,* I convinced myself. *I must show them that I am okay. God promised that he would take care of me, and he will give me the strength.*

I showed up at the event, and several women sauntered up to talk with me. "I have nothing to hide," I told them boldly. "I'm an innocent woman."

After Mike was well enough to live on his own, I landed a new job as a clerical worker in Concord and relocated. Trying to save money, I moved in with two roommates. I continued partying hard and using drugs. Deep down, I knew it wasn't the healthiest behavior, but the drugs temporarily helped me escape my troubles and forget about the murder charges. But I never forgot about God and the promise he'd given me in that parking lot.

One night, emotionally exhausted, I cried out to God. "I don't want to do this anymore! But I don't want to spend the rest of my life in prison. Please, help me!"

The next morning, someone pounded on the front door of my house. I opened it and found a police officer standing there.

"Can I come in and search your house?" he asked.

SECOND CHANCES

"Sure." I shrugged. "I have nothing to hide. I do have two roommates, though, and I'm not responsible for their stuff."

Another police officer followed him, and they tore through the house, looking in every corner and closet. They arrested my roommates and hauled them away. To my relief, they turned to me and said, "We wrote everything up. You are free to go."

I let out the breath I'd been holding the whole time and bid them goodbye. After closing the door, I sank onto the couch. *Oh, man, I can't do this anymore. God, I am done with this life. This is just too hectic and exhausting. I am done with it for good.*

My boss at the clerical company approached me one day not long after. "Bethany, I'd love it if you would go to church with me and my wife sometime," he said with a smile.

"Yeah, that sounds great." *Church. Wow, I haven't set foot in church in years.* I knew my boss was a Christian, and he and his wife expressed a deep faith in God. They talked of becoming missionaries, sharing about God with people in another country. I admired them and their values. Perhaps going to church wouldn't be such a bad thing. After all, I'd just told God I was done with my lifestyle. Perhaps this was all part of his rescue plan.

I walked through the doors of their church the following Sunday, not sure what to expect. I had not been to church since going with my sister years before. *What will people think of me?* I thought with uncertainty as I sat down. *What if they knew the life I've lived? A life of drugs, motorcycle gangs and even being accused of murder? Would they still want to get to know me?*

To my surprise, I enjoyed the service more than I thought I would. The pastor spoke about God's love, reminding us that there was nothing that could ever make God stop loving us. We simply had to turn from our wrongdoings and give our hearts over to him.

The message resonated with me. *I do want to believe that you love me, God, that you still care about me. I have seen your provision over the years, and I know that you have not forgotten me. I've screwed up plenty of times, but I still believe that you have a plan for my life. You rescued me from death years ago in that hospital room, and you did it again when I had my son. You spared his life in that motorcycle crash as well. I know that you care, and I want to make things right. Please forgive me for the wrong I've done.*

I continued going to church on and off with my boss and his wife. Slowly, I connected the gospel message of the Bible with what God was showing me in my heart. I'd learned as a young girl that God had sent his son, Jesus, to earth to die for the wrong things we'd done. Because of his sacrificial act, we could spend eternity in heaven with God if we surrendered our lives to him. He loved us, and he wanted a relationship with us. I'd always believed in God and prayed to him, but I hadn't always followed or trusted him. I'd used him as a lifeline, grabbing on to him as I swung over treacherous waters below. He had rescued me at my most dire moments and given me a second chance. But now I truly wanted to live for him. I did not have my future entirely figured out, but I would trust that he had a plan.

My faith was soon put to the test. New management took over my company, and I lost my job. The news devastated me, but I did not come unglued. I had been learning to trust in God for the big and small details in my life, and I knew he would provide another opportunity.

I gave up the drugs for good and focused on rebuilding my life. My daughter suggested I try Celebration Church, where she attended.

"I think you will really like it, Mom," she said. Now married with children of her own, she had made a great life for herself, and I was very proud of her.

"All right. I'll check it out," I agreed.

I checked out Celebration Church off and on and enjoyed it, but I still wasn't certain I wanted to commit.

"Just keep going every single week," my daughter encouraged me.

I did as she said, and within no time, the church began to feel like home. Every time I walked through the doors, someone greeted me with a warm hug or a smile. It felt nice to be noticed and loved. I had spent years living in loneliness with no one to lean on during difficult times. I'd learned the hard way that my partying friends from the bars weren't true friends — they were simply out for a good time and a few drinks. But here, something felt different. These people genuinely loved God, and they genuinely loved me. And that was something I had not felt in a very long while.

I began getting involved at church, helping out in any way I could. As I did, God began to do an amazing work in my heart. I realized that I had spent my whole life trying to do things my way instead of his way. Now, for the first time, I began to truly listen to his direction. As I surrendered my life to him, he clearly showed me the way. I no longer needed to live in fear, because I knew that he had a plan.

I landed a job as an apartment manager, but the job soon proved tedious. I worked around the clock, as tenants came knocking at my door at all hours of the day and night. I soon began to feel trapped and unhappy, and others noticed. *I don't know how much longer I can keep this up,* I thought, exhausted. *I've just got to keep pressing on until I find something else.*

I continued to pray, asking God to help me find a better job. Just when I thought I could not take it anymore, he provided an amazing opportunity. I landed another job as an apartment manager, working a manageable 20 hours per week. The owner and his wife proved to be wonderful people who showered me with unconditional love. *Thank you, God,* I prayed. *You are so good, so faithful! You have provided above and beyond what I dreamed of. You always take care of my needs. I will never stop trusting in you.*

❧❧❧

SECOND CHANCES

"Come on, Charles, let's go." I gave my dog a playful pat, and he hopped off the bed and bounded out of the room. I followed after him, and we headed outside for a brisk morning walk. Up above, the sun started to poke out from behind the clouds, promising a beautiful, sunny day. As Charles trotted in front of me, I ran after him and laughed. *After 14 years, you still keep me on my toes, ol' boy.*

Though God is all powerful and Charles is my furry companion, I can't help but think of God's unconditional love when I spend time with Charles. My dog is always there to greet me when I walk in the door, an eager smile on his face. He follows me wherever I go, never leaving my side. No matter what I do, he loves me just the same. There is nothing I can do to make Charles stop loving me. Nor is there anything I can do to make God stop loving me.

My life has been a nonstop adventure in the past few years. Five years ago, my daughter, her four children and her husband moved to Idaho. I miss her and talk with her often, so grateful for her faith and her maturity. My son has held a steady job since high school and just bought his first house. Though once a victim of a horrific motorcycle crash, he races motorcycles today and has no fear of the bikes. I am very proud of him.

Mike and I remain close friends. I have never remarried, but he has been a constant companion by my side all these years. He has learned to get around on one leg and does not let his handicap keep him from enjoying life. In regards to finding a new husband, I have told God many times, "If you don't pick him, I don't have him." I am confident that if he wants me to remarry, he will bring someone along. In the meantime, I trust in his timing.

My father passed away three years ago. He lived a difficult life, and my heart went out to him. I have kept in touch with most of my siblings, and we remain as close as possible, despite the distance. Though we are all different in our own ways, we are still family, and nothing can break that bond.

I continue my involvement at Celebration Church and cannot think of anywhere else I'd rather be. I now understand what fellowship means. It is a beautiful connection of people who love God, all living life together. We each face struggles, but we do not face them alone. At last, I have a group of friends I can completely rely on. I have enjoyed being a part of several ministries at the church, putting my time to use in a positive way.

Through the wonderful teaching at my church, I have learned about God's deep, intimate love for each of us. I spent years searching for acceptance and love, wondering why people always seemed to let me down. But God has reminded me through the Bible that he loves me just as I am and that he has loved me long before I even came to know him. My favorite verse, Psalm 139, remains permanently pressed on my heart: "O Lord, you have searched me and you know me. You know when I sit and when I rise. You perceive my thoughts from afar. You discern my going out and my lying down. You are familiar with all my ways … For you created my inmost being, you knit me together in my mother's womb. I praise you because I am wonderfully and fearfully made … All the days ordained for me were written in your book before one of them came to be."

It comforts me greatly to think that God has known every single one of my thoughts and every day of my life. He is the only constant in this ever-changing world.

Once upon a time, as a frightened 15-year-old little girl in a hospital Intensive Care Unit, I fought for my life. But as I began to slip into eternity, an angel stopped me with an important message: "It is not your time." Even when I did not know him, God was making plans for me. He still had work for me to do on earth.

Today, God is still making those plans for me. He has rescued me out of a lifestyle of loneliness, drugs and destruction and planted me in a wonderful church. He has provided true friends who care about me and pray for me. Most importantly, he has mended my broken heart. He has shown me unconditional love and given me a faithful companion in Charles to remind me daily of that love. Though the rest of my days remain uncertain, I do not worry. I trust in him and know his path is always best. He will not let me down, and he will never let me go.

TOOLS OF THE TRADE
THE STORY OF DOUG
WRITTEN BY LORI MCCLURE

I walked into the courthouse nervous and unsure about what the final outcome would be. Various family members, including Mom and Dad, waited right outside the courtroom. Silence greeted me in the awkward moment, and no words seemed adequate.

Today I would find out just how much time I could spend with my two daughters in the future, if any at all. The custody battle between me and Sharon divided my family — even my own parents planned to testify against me, to convince the judge of my unfit parental status and to brand me an alcoholic and drug addict. Even though some of my extended family members agreed to testify as character witnesses for me, my parents' rejection still stung.

We all stood quiet with emotions raw and faces red. I wondered what the next few moments would bring, but before words were spoken that no one could take back, a settlement was reached. No one had to testify or take sides. Nevertheless, the thought of never seeing my girls again, of how close I came to that awful reality, scared me. I wondered if I could ever truly make the changes necessary to turn my life around.

STRUCK

❧ ❧ ❧

Mom's overprotective nature stifled me. Maybe it was because I spent so many days sick as a kid, but once I felt well, nothing could stop me, except for the occasional need for stitches. My energy never ended, and my fearless nature kept me constantly exploring and pushing right past the boundaries Mom set for me.

Even though I feared little, the awkward process of moving between 17 different schools in 17 years left me frustrated much of the time. In the worst school year, we moved three times, and I never got used to the misery of starting over.

Dad worked as a carpenter, so we relocated to wherever he found work. I understood, but I also hated the process of meeting new people only to start over again in a few months. Making connections proved close to impossible, and eventually I stopped trying. My personality shifted from outgoing to subdued as I sought to blend in as much as possible while staying under the radar.

I tried smoking pot for the first time as a sophomore in high school. I embraced the change it brought to my perceptions, and it helped me relax around others. A bunch of high school footballers lit up while crammed into a car on the way to a party, and I enjoyed being a part of something, a team, a group. Being a big guy, football suited me, and recruiters were even seeking me out for baseball. I played first base and could hit really well, but I wanted freedom, and the only thought on my mind was breaking out of my small town.

As soon as graduation came, I rushed headfirst into life and left for the big city of Portland. I mowed grass and spread bark dust for money and spent the weekends partying at the river with cousins and friends. I had a strong work ethic, having worked for my uncle bucking hay to buy school clothes for myself, but I also craved the easygoing party life.

Partying with others gave me a common ground to build on, a way to relate without really having to know each other. Everyone sought to escape from something, and we all escaped together. But after a steady stream of partying for several months, I decided to get serious and move on with my life. Trade school seemed the best answer for me.

I chose to attend Universal Technical Institute to study heating, refrigeration, air conditioning and solar energy. The eight-month program appealed to me much more than a standard four-year college program. The school offered job placement services, another added bonus. I traveled to Phoenix to start my studies, and suddenly I found myself surrounded by a group of guys, 99 percent of whom seemed to spend their free time drinking and doing drugs.

I learned about meth at trade school. Bound by the pressure and weight of exceeding and succeeding, we all hung out, drank heavily and used drugs regularly. One night my roommate gave me a small line of meth, and I marveled at the ability the drug gave me to drink and still feel in control.

Soon I started selling drugs on the side for extra money because everyone needed a dealer. Being able to provide what everyone wanted made me appealing to others in a way I'd never been before. I liked it. I sold to everyone, even one of my instructors.

At trade school, drugs were a lifestyle, not just a weekend thing, and everyone had the common goal of distraction. I liked who I became while I used, too. My personality opened up, and life was fun again. I was fun.

Despite my lifestyle, I managed to graduate with solid grades, and I had no trouble finding work. I moved back to Portland and got a job with a maintenance company taking care of marinas, docks and houseboat electrical issues. I spent the first few months learning the ropes, but I excelled quickly. Things were going great until I got a ticket while driving the company van, and insurance refused to cover me anymore. The company fired me.

My cousin helped me get another job as a laborer on a construction site for $5 an hour. It wasn't much, but I needed the job. Being a third-generation carpenter gave me a natural ability for driving nails. I excelled at framing, and I took pride in being able to complete a whole job with little help from others. I went from being a skinny meth-head kid to a capable man with big, strong arms.

But every person I met used drugs on this new job site, so I returned to a similar culture as trade school again. Between pot and meth, we were high most of the time, and things went downhill fast. I stopped taking care of myself, and I often wound up in situations that were out of control. With so many people high everywhere I went, the atmosphere usually pulsed with potential for trouble. Multiple times guns were pulled on or near me when things got heated between angry dealers and users. The goal switched from fun to survival.

I took too many conflicting substances trying to keep up with everyone, and my body was confused. I found myself hallucinating, seeing monsters out of the corner of my eye. Sweat poured off my body, and I came close to overdosing more than once. I decided to quit meth, even though I kept smoking pot and drinking.

ॐॐॐ

I met Sharon at the age of 23, and our relationship was purely physical. We moved in together quickly, and two months later, she became pregnant. Fatherhood seemed so far removed from where I was in my life, considering that my buddy and I were selling pot out of the back bedroom. I didn't know how to handle the situation.

"What do you want to do, Sharon?"

"I don't know."

"Should we get married? Is that what you want?" We were not in love, even though we were bound together by this new life forming inside of her. When she agreed to marry me, I freaked out inside, but I didn't back out. We married and bought a house.

STRUCK

Sharon gave birth to our first daughter, and I had no clue how to be a dad or husband. All I knew how to do was work, drink, sell pot and get high. Our marriage consisted of little more than fighting, and I knew nothing of how to love. I grew up on job sites and learned how to treat a woman from the dirt bags I worked with. Their advice only hurt my marriage further when I followed it.

In the midst of our tumultuous marriage, our second daughter was born, and I marveled at how beautiful both my daughters turned out. How could I be a part of creating such perfect girls? I couldn't believe how perfect they were, considering all the substances I consumed. The girls were the only good things about Sharon and me. We couldn't make it work, and our divorce came when our girls were 3 and 4.

Sharon quickly met someone new, and I hated the thought of another man raising my daughters. My life floundered as I struggled both privately and professionally. Disappointed in my job prospects, I started my own business, despite my lack of management skills. My mistakes piled higher and higher. I kept track of nothing and failed to file taxes for 10 years. Even though I was doing everything wrong, it took a while to catch up with me.

Sharon and I reunited for the sake of our girls, and I worked like a madman framing houses by myself. I did the work of a four-man crew alone. I felt like Superman. Even though my capabilities allowed me to work myself into the ground, the consequence of my independent work schedule included much physical pain. Smoking pot brought relief. My body began to fall apart. Between street drugs and prescription drugs, illicit substances continually coursed through my veins.

My health took a turn for the worse when I contracted a staph infection in my knee from kneeling on top plates at work. Metal pieces had worked their way under my skin and caused an infection, and the antibiotics were rendered useless by my drinking and substance abuse.

The doctor performed a surgical procedure to scrape the infection out of my knee. The process proved much more taxing than I anticipated, and I couldn't work for a month. Once I did return to work, I found myself hurt again on the job when I broke several ribs. Worried about mounting bills, I pushed myself to go back to work in two weeks. Again, smoking pot eased the pain. Every inhalation helped to numb my lungs so I could breathe easier.

Life continued to disappoint as my marriage settled into old behaviors, and Sharon I couldn't stop fighting. We were miserable and unhappy, and when I met a new girl at my brother's wedding, I slipped right into a relationship with her without thinking twice. A month later, we moved in together, and Sharon, fueled by hurt and anger, threatened to make sure I never saw the girls again. I knew my lack of morals failed me in my relationships, but I still had pride in my ability to work hard.

Even though my work ethic seemed solid in my mind,

money slipped through my fingers. I rushed to buy a new truck before the custody issue got further down the road. But even that ended poorly when the transmission broke 19 miles into my ownership. A month later, the distributor broke. Work dried up, and the amount of child support I owed rolled in at $686 per month. I couldn't pay it.

While I refused to pay child support, the fees racked up, and within two years, I owed $30,000 in back child support. My benefits and business license were revoked, so even if there was work to be done, I could never make the same amount of money as before. Now even my work and financial life were in ruins. I had nothing to hold onto, and it seemed life kept handing me more than my fair share of misfortune. I kept coasting. I saw no way to make things better with such insurmountable obstacles before me.

I found work with a friend detailing cars, and I did side jobs and piecework here and there, but the money didn't add up. My poor choices had ruined my life. My short-lived relationship ended, but a new one popped up to take its place with a much younger girl, Ashley, who was in her 20s.

After only a couple of months, Ashley told me she was pregnant with my child, and her eyes were now opened to my bad influence in her life. She sobered up, but I didn't, so I became the last person she wanted to be around anymore. She gave birth to a son I never saw because her mom and dad took her away and made sure I wouldn't find them. The most horrible feeling pooled in the pit of my stomach. I had a son I would never know.

Everything slipped through my fingers. Owing back child support even cost me my driver's license. I crashed with friends and family. I fought to see my girls. The only steady parts of my life became cigarettes, meth, alcohol and pot. I still managed to meet a new girl named Cynthia, who I dated for two months. She disappeared only to return a month later.

"I'm pregnant, Doug," she said.

"Oh." *Why was she telling me?* "Who's the father?" My question started a floodgate of tears from her, and I realized my mistake. Obviously, I had my answer: She thought I was the father. We moved in together but didn't marry. My mountain of financial debt resulted in a week of jail time. When I got out, an ankle bracelet kept me in line for a month. Life continued in its chaotic path. Our son, Caleb, was born, and I breathed a sigh of relief when he came out looking exactly like me. He really was mine.

But a new son didn't stop the mess of our lives. Cynthia had anger issues. Even anger management classes couldn't stop her episodes of rage. Our fights turned violent on her part and ended with 911 calls because it was the only way I could get her to stop hitting me. But this madness became our life. I sat in it for so long, I became used to it. I never could have predicted the next turn our lives would take.

❧ ❧ ❧

"I'm changed! Doug, wake up! I've changed." Cynthia's excitement woke me out of a deep sleep, and I groggily stared at her.

"Good for you. I'm going back to sleep." I turned to get comfortable once again and laid my head back on my pillow.

"No, you don't get it. I quit smoking. I'm changed!"

"You're right. I don't get it, and I'm going back to sleep."

"No, listen, we need to get married." That phrase woke me up fast.

"Seriously? What are you talking about, Cynthia?"

"We need to get our lives together for our children, Doug. God changed me, and I want to go to church as a family."

"Are you kidding me right now? Church is full of hypocrites! Why would you want that for yourself or the kids? There's no point to any of it. Besides, I've done that before. I don't want to do it again."

I knew about church. My parents used to drag me there when I was a kid. We went all the time. Dad was a deacon. Mom played the piano. Every time the doors opened, we went.

I learned all the Bible stories they taught in Sunday school. I knew how to find a scripture quickly, thanks to the games we played where you had to be the first one to find a particular Bible reference. Yes, I knew about church. I knew about God. But mostly, I knew how to sit in the back row pretending to stay awake during church. That's what I remembered most. And now, just as then, I had no interest in going to church with Cynthia or in taking our kids.

The next Sunday, I woke up to smoke a joint as usual before my first morning cup of coffee. All the kids were with us for the weekend — my two daughters, Cynthia's son from a previous marriage and Caleb. Cynthia got ready and started to get the kids ready, while I sat around in my bathrobe enjoying my buzz.

"Where are you going?" I asked.

"I'm going to church, like I said I was, and I'm taking the kids."

"Well, the Sunday school part is for kids, so you guys go. Have fun." Even though church didn't appeal to me, and I believed the majority of church people to be hypocrites, I felt guilty. But I couldn't go to church high. I sat alone feeling pretty low at the thought of Cynthia taking the kids to church alone. I got up, got dressed and took the bus to church.

I sneaked into the back row of the church feeling uncomfortable and sure I would see someone from my past. The odds were good I'd run into a person I had fought with, slept with, worked with or even sold drugs to. I sat still, afraid of finding a familiar face, so I made eye contact with no one. When Sunday school ended, Cynthia came out surprised and excited to see me. We sat, and I listened to the preacher as he talked about David and Goliath. My focus drifted in and out, just waiting for the end of the service so I could rush out the back door. I stood with the rest of the congregation as the final songs played. I inched closer to the exit. They sang and prayed, and I grew more and more fidgety, hoping for the end to finally come.

Cynthia grabbed my hand and walked me down the aisle. *Maybe she wants to introduce me to someone,* I thought. But she kept walking nearer to the front where people stood praying. When I realized she was leading me there as well, the door felt a million miles away. I stood uncomfortable and uneasy as the pastor came over to me and put his hand on my chest. He prayed, and I didn't think much about his words.

The service ended, and we gathered the kids into the van and headed to Mom's. My thoughts focused on only one thing: I couldn't breathe.

"Are you all right?"

"Yeah, I'm okay." I tried to play it off, to be cool, but I couldn't breathe. My chest hurt. I composed myself as we walked into Mom's house. I walked around trying to shake off the pain and suffocation I felt. In an instant of inexplicable change, a weight lifted off me, which was replaced with the calmest sense of peace and love and acceptance washing down over me. I felt good in a way I never had before. I'd gotten high many times, but I'd never felt a high like this. Peace and love and acceptance. I felt it all in one moment, and I turned to my mom and said, "I'm changed."

"What?"

"I'm changed. We went to church, and God changed

me, Mom. Something is different now. The pastor prayed for me, and now I can feel that I'm not the same man."

The weights lifted off, and I knew God had done a work in me that would change my life forever. For 13 years, a little plastic bag had been a constant answer in my front pocket. I'd reach my hand down just to feel the plastic hope against my fingers, to know my escape was moments away, the release I needed. But I knew, in that moment, I needed it no more. I realized the fog had lifted forever. God had calmed me in a way that no substance had ever been able to do. I felt true freedom for the first time in my life.

I went back to the same church again that night. At the end of the service, I made my way to the front for more prayer, because I wanted to get rid of the fear, anger and lust that had controlled me my whole life. I wanted whatever Jesus had, so I prayed to God and gave him all of me. "Lord, you know who I am. You know what I've done. I know you've changed me. Whatever you need from me? You've got it."

I couldn't understand why Jesus would change me, why he would bother doing anything for someone like me. Other people might deserve to be forgiven, to be loved and changed. I knew I didn't deserve it. All I had to give in return was my life.

Cynthia and I got married in the same church three days later. Things were better in many ways, but she still struggled with issues from her childhood. She had also been diagnosed with bipolar disorder, but she wouldn't take her medicine. She managed to stay sober for a long time, but eventually alcohol became the comfort she turned to for relief from her symptoms.

I kept close to God, praying as much as I could and reading my Bible. My parents returned to church when they saw the change in me. I thought back to the moment when my relationship with my parents had been so strained. They were ready to testify against me in court because of my actions. And now we were going to church together. God provided this blessing of a mended relationship.

The first time Mom came with me, she had an experience that was very much out of her comfort zone. She grew up as a Southern Baptist and was rather conservative. Many times she even made fun of "holy rollers," people who seemed to experience God in charismatic and emotional ways. But that day at church, the pastor walked down the aisle, took her hand, touched her head and she fell down on the ground. I saw a difference in her life after that experience.

I called my dad and spoke to him about God. "Dad, it says here in the Bible that if you're lukewarm the Lord will spew you out of his mouth. I have no idea where you land when he spews you out of his mouth. Wouldn't it be better not to find out?"

My parents started going to church regularly, and I continued to change, to look for ways to grow. I truly believed my life belonged to Christ now. Whatever the pastor needed, whatever God needed, I gave it. When I couldn't find work, I showed up at the church to volunteer. For the next year, I went through a home study course for ministry. I learned everything I could as quickly as I could.

Financially, things weren't going well, and I was arrested for not paying child support. Discouragement settled in, and when I got out of jail, Cynthia said she didn't want to continue our marriage. All my stuff was already out of the house, and I moved in with my family.

Even though Cynthia struggled, I forgave her because I knew how many mistakes I had made in my past. I went back to her and tried to help her. I took her to a program called Celebrate Recovery. When I moved Cynthia to a more remote place with less opportunity for drinking and temptation, we started going to the Celebration Church in Fairfield. I tried to create an environment she could survive and thrive in. We moved to a place with trees all around where I thought peace might come easier. For the next year, Cynthia tried, but she wasn't doing well, and she filed for divorce.

Devastated by another unwelcome change in my life, I searched for relief at Celebration Church. There was so much love there. It still took me more than a year to recover. The pain and hurt from the divorce, from all the choices I had made, took time to fade. But Celebration Church was a place of safety and comfort for me. I felt free to take the time I needed to recover from a lifetime of hurt.

When I met Tiffany, I couldn't believe the love that

was possible between two people. We met and married, and this marriage was different because I believe God brought her to me. This marriage held everything that had been absent in my past relationships: trust, unconditional love, joy. For the first time in my life, I understood love. I desired to love and be loved.

I'm still learning to love, still growing every day. I'm thankful God sent me to Celebration Church, because it's a place filled with people who demonstrate continual love. Between Tiffany and my church family, I have matured from that boy forever stuck at 17 into a man able to accept God's love, receive Tiffany's love and give love right back to both of them.

In addition to finding this new love, I found a way to share the changes God made in my life with the guys I worked with. Just like the old me, I still found others desperate for relief from the emptiness of a life searching for meaning. Sharing about the new man God made me helped give hope to others whose only solution was to drown their pain in alcohol and drug use, as I had done for so many years. Now I had a lasting solution to offer.

I'd spent my whole life trying to live and love without the right tools of the trade, and now that I had them, I determined to build my life on a foundation much bigger than my own self and desires. I want to build on the foundation of God and his love, because after all, Jesus was the ultimate carpenter with the best tools of all — acceptance, peace and love.

REVEALING THE TRUTH
THE STORY OF BELLE
WRITTEN BY ALEXINE GARCIA

"He's cheated on me!" I cried into the phone.

Between sobs, Marvin tried to calm me down. "Wait, stop yelling, Belle. I can barely understand you." I sobbed into my palm and tried to calm down. I wiped my eyes with the collar of my shirt.

"He slept with someone else," I whispered between sobs.

"How do you know for sure?"

"We got into a huge fight, and he admitted to it."

"Well, what are you going to do? Why don't you come stay with me?"

"I drove back to Vacaville. I was going to go to my mom's house, but she's just going to tell me she knew this would happen. I just don't need to hear that right now. I'm in a hotel room."

"Tell me where you are, and I'll be right over," he said softly. I needed comfort. The thought of crying in my friend's arms to soothe my pain sounded comforting.

"Okay."

The next morning I stood at the window wrapped in hotel sheets, watching the sun come up. I looked back at Marvin still asleep in the bed. I felt shame crawl over my skin. I was no better than Fred.

STRUCK

❧❧❧

The first thing I saw was the bouquet of flowers sitting on the coffee table as I walked into the apartment. Part of me felt relieved, but I was still hurt. This meant I wouldn't have to admit what happened with Marvin. I loved Fred, and I just couldn't lose him, and now I wouldn't have to. Fred came out of the bedroom still wearing the same clothes from the day before. His hair was uncombed and wild. He took two steps across the tiny apartment and grabbed me up in a hug. "I'm so sorry," he whispered. He held me at arm's length and looked me in the eyes as he fell to his knees and apologized over and over.

A few weeks later, I sat on the edge of the bed and looked down at the little blue plus sign. My heart raced. I was 18. I had two jobs, which was just barely covering our rent, while Fred was in and out of jobs. *What in the world am I going to do?* My mind went fuzzy, and I could hear my heart beating in my ears as I wondered whose baby this was.

Karen came over for lunch, and I showed her the test. We looked over the hotel receipt from the night with Marvin, and the dates just didn't line up. There really was no way this could be Marvin's baby. This was perfect for me because I was sure I loved Fred. He was my life. Even the doctor's estimate of the date of conception seemed to rule out Marvin as the father. When Scotty was born two weeks late, I was certain that Fred was the father.

Marvin's mother, Mary, had a special love for me and continued to talk to me, even after the whole mess settled. When Fred decided he wanted nothing to do with the delivery, Mary offered to be my coach and stay with me every moment of the way.

After Scotty's birth, Mary invited me to a family barbeque, and I saw it as a chance to get away for a bit. Fred's constant drinking and partying was wearing me down, and I needed a breath of fresh air.

"Would you like a steak or a hamburger, darling?" Mary asked. It was a beautiful summer day, and everyone was smiling and laughing.

"A hamburger is fine."

"I'll hold Scotty," Marvin said as he took Scotty carefully from my arms. Scotty was growing so fast. He hadn't learned to speak yet, but he would make sounds and laugh and giggle.

"You know, Marvin, Scotty kind of looks like you," his cousin, Jenna, remarked. I was so insulted, I nearly dropped my plate.

"How could you say something so disrespectful?" I said in shock. "That's Fred's baby; don't you forget it."

෴෴෴

I fumbled with the keys in one hand and Scotty in the other as I came back in the apartment. When I opened the door, I was greeted by a group of Fred's friends laughing and drinking at the dinner table. A fog of smoke and the thick dank smell of weed filled the tiny apartment. I could tolerate this. But it was the blue broken bits of the piggy bank that drew a scowl on my face. Fred had smashed the bank full of Scotty's pennies to gamble with his friends. I guess he needed every cent he could get to go out and buy some more weed.

"I'd like you and your friends to wrap this up." I glared at him as I slammed the bedroom door behind me. I changed Scotty into his pajamas and put him to bed. The apartment grew quiet, and I was relieved to have them gone. I quietly left Scotty sleeping as I went back to the kitchen. The mess of beer bottles and poker chips and cards were left, but my boyfriend was gone.

I only stayed for a little bit longer, and then I decided to move in with my mother. I'd had enough. I was working in a restaurant and at a gas station. I met my next roommate, John, while pumping gas. He drove the Pepsi trucks and made regular stops at our station. John was into drugs, too, mainly meth, but he seemed more responsible about it.

"Have you ever tried this stuff?" he offered.

"No, I've never done any drugs. You know I don't party."

"Well, this is different. It's not a downer like pot. This is an upper. You'll be up for days, just high on life," he said with a smile. This sounded so appealing to me. Working two jobs and trying to raise my son was really burning me out. Maybe this was just what I needed to keep me going. All it took was a little coaxing, and I was hooked. I never considered myself addicted because I didn't need it every day. The long hours at work became more bearable.

About a month later, I was so relieved when I got a job at the post office. It was an hour away, in Oakland, but it was the beginning of a wonderful career, or so I thought. I began leaving Scotty in Fairfield with my mother, then driving to Oakland to work and then back home to Napa. I could work the long hours, drive the long hours and sleep as little as possible to make it all work with the help of meth. Driving to pick up Scotty and driving back home was not as hard when I was wide-awake and smiling.

I was on a 12-hour shift taking a break from the mail sorter one night when a tall, handsome man came by on a mail carrier. I was blown away by his smile and dark, handsome eyes.

"How are you doing tonight?"

"I'm hanging in there. Just a few more hours till my shift ends."

"My name's Henry," he said, extending his hand.

"Nice to meet you. I'm Belle."

৵৵৵

Moving in with Henry was the best decision possible, or so I thought. Henry was loving and caring. He went the extra mile to make sure I was taken care of. He provided for Scotty and me, and he was so hardworking.

One Saturday morning I got Scotty dressed and ready to see his father. I could see a snap of excitement in his eyes. He was only 2, but he had an understanding of what was going on.

I knocked on the apartment door, and Fred answered with that familiar disheveled look. He was shirtless with pajama pants and messy hair. I could tell by the look on his face that he had completely forgotten about the scheduled visit that day.

He walked back into the dark apartment and said, "Come in," over his shoulder.

"I can see you just woke up." The place had the familiar dank smell and décor of empty beer cans.

"Are you gonna nag on me like old times?" he asked, rubbing his eyes. "I don't have to listen to you anymore, Belle."

"No, but you still have a son to father."

"Yeah, well, we're gonna have to do this another day because I don't feel up to babysitting today."

I didn't say another word. I didn't even look at him as I walked out the door. I could see all of Scotty's excitement deflate. As we walked back in our apartment, Henry must have seen it, too.

"What happened?"

I gave him a look to let him know this was not the time to discuss it. He took Scotty in his arms and walked into the bathroom. He stood him up on the toilet and stooped down to look Scotty in the eyes.

"Look, son. From here on out, I'm going to be your dad. You don't have to worry about anything because I'm going to take care of you." Scotty wrapped his arms around Henry's neck in a huge hug. I felt relief rush through my heart as the two embraced. I really thought this was going to be the beginning of something great.

As I walked down the aisle to marry Henry, I could see my Happily Ever After forming. I felt like a Disney princess finally getting my chance at happiness, a family and love. Henry's son, Joseph, became part of our family, too. We both continued to work at the post office on the graveyard shift. It was nice being together all the time.

I was driving home one cold, rainy night with no moon in sight. My eyelids were wide open because of the meth in my system, and I sped down the freeway, music blasting. I was passing the Berkley Racetrack when all of a sudden I lost control of my car. My head went dizzy as the car spun in circles. *I'm going to die high on drugs,* is what ran through my mind in that swift moment. The car came to a halt as I pushed my foot down onto the brakes. I looked around at the cold, dark night. Had I died in that moment, the autopsy would show the drugs in my system, and my son would be forever scarred. As my pulse slowed and I calmed down, I made the decision never to touch meth again.

Things were getting better and better. Now after nine months of drug abuse, I was clean and still able to manage my life. One day, the silver lining threatened to fade. I was picking Scotty up from my mom's house when she pulled me into the kitchen.

"Do you leave your son alone with Henry?" she whispered. I was stunned.

"Of course I do, he's Scotty's stepdad. What are you trying to say?"

"I'm not saying anything. Your son is the one talking. Today he told me that Henry pushed him into the wall for no good reason."

"Oh, Mother, I don't think there's anything to worry about. Henry would never hurt Scotty. He calls him Dad. They love each other."

"Well, Belle, how do you explain this?" As Scotty walked in the room, she lifted his sleeve revealing a bruise.

"They were probably roughhousing. You know kids exaggerate. I need to get going, Mom." I was so insulted.

In 1990, as I became pregnant with my second child, a small, steady worry began to form. I knew Henry had two other kids from two different women, but I was the one he married. I was his special princess, and things were different this time. However, the worry sat in the back of my mind.

As I was working the mail sorter one night, Christina came up to me. "Is it time for your break yet?" I looked back at the clock.

"I just need another two minutes," I shouted over the noise.

"I'll meet you in the break room."

I filled up my coffee mug before sitting down with her. "How are things going in your department?"

"We've only got a 10-minute break, so I'm going to get straight to the point, Belle." The look in her eyes was intense. I could see she had something really important to say to me. "Have you noticed anything funny about Henry?"

Her question hit me like a punch to the throat. I began to wonder if people just couldn't stand to see someone happy.

"What are you trying to imply, Christina?"

"A couple of us have seen Henry with another woman. He doesn't even try to hide it, Belle."

"Thank you, Christina, but me and Henry are just fine." I got up from the table and went back to mail sorting.

Soon after, I was driving Scotty home from my mom's house. There was a bottle of fancy lotion in the cup holder. At first I thought maybe this was a gift for me, but then I saw it was half used. It reminded me of the type you get in hotel rooms. Another time it was a button, and I even found a lipstick case. I chose to push all this to the back of my mind. I literally ignored it.

In March 1991, our second son, Adam, was born. A week later, I found out he had a genetic metabolic disorder called PKU, and my entire life changed in an instant.

"Your baby will need a special diet and special care for a very long time," the nurse told us. I began making regular visits to the hospital in San Francisco. As he grew, I had to calculate every bit of food he ate to make sure he didn't eat too much protein. I balanced his diet, just like balancing a checkbook. He became my number one job. I kept a journal of his weight and diet. I quit my job at the post office to take care of Adam full time.

STRUCK

❧❧❧

Things began to settle down, and I was really getting the hang of watching over Adam and maintaining his diet. One summer afternoon we invited our families over for a barbeque to celebrate my mom's and aunt's birthdays. It was a bright, sunny day, and the kids were running around playing.

Everyone seemed to be having fun, but there was an obvious tension in the air. My mother was always cautious around Henry. And Henry was uneasy with Adam's diet. He couldn't stand the fact that his son would never be able to eat meat.

I watched as he drank one beer after the other. I smiled and laughed with our guests, but on the inside, my heart was beating wildly.

I was relieved when everyone left. I took Henry upstairs because he was too drunk to walk on his own. He felt heavier and more unsteady with each stair. When we got to the bedroom, I took off his shoes and jeans and laid him in the bed. I made sure to turn him on his side in case he started vomiting.

Although I was exhausted, I went back to the kitchen and began cleaning and washing the dishes. It was nice to be alone in the quiet, or so I thought. I didn't even hear him come downstairs. He was suddenly behind me yelling.

"I know you're seeing someone behind my back!"

"What are you talking about? That's not true," I answered in shock.

REVEALING THE TRUTH

"Don't lie to me. I know you are seeing someone." His rage was written all over his red face. He lurched at me and grabbed me by the arms. Before I knew it, I was being shoved into the pantry closet.

"You are drunk. Just go back upstairs, and go to bed!" I shouted, two inches from his face. This only woke his rage even more. He began punching me as hard as he could. I lifted my arms to cover my face and backed into the corner.

"Please stop!" I shouted between sobs. "Please, I love you, I'm not cheating." Either he got tired or he finally listened to me and stopped. He left me there in the pantry, and I ran to the phone to call my mother.

"What do you think you are doing?" He snatched the phone from my hand.

"I need to get some help. I'm going to call my mom."

"You're not calling anyone. You're gonna sit there and think about what you did to me." Out of desperation, I fell to my knees and begged him.

"Please, Henry, please let me call my mom. I'm in so much pain."

"You know what, you're right. I just want you out of here. I'll call her myself." He punched the keys so hard he nearly broke the phone.

"You need to come pick up your daughter," is all I heard as I cried.

❧❧❧

"Do you want to press charges?" the doctor asked me. The hospital room was cold and stark white. My head was throbbing from the bruise on my scalp.

"No. No, I don't," I whispered.

"Sweetie, he fractured your nose, and you're covered in bruises. Are you sure this is the right choice?" my mom asked me.

"Mom, I just want to go home. I want to work this out." At that point, even with every ounce drained from me and all of my body aching, I thought that I could make our marriage work.

"I'm so sorry," Henry said over the phone. "I don't remember any of it." I could hear him holding back tears. I drove over to the house because I wanted him to look at me and see what he had done to me. Had anyone else put me through this, Henry would have been enraged. I walked in the front door. As I stood in front of him, I saw the color leave his face. I knew then that he was telling the truth about the blackout.

"Oh, my God, Belle, I am so sorry. Please come home. Give me another chance," he said, shaking his head.

"I'm only going to come back if you go to counseling. We have issues that need to be worked out."

"At this point, I'll do anything. I just want to be together." His pitiful pleas were enough for me.

When I moved back in, Henry's dad started picking up Scotty and Adam for church every Sunday. He even came when Joseph was not with us, which I thought showed his true feelings for our family. Even though Scotty was not his biological grandson, he cared deeply about him. I even started going to Bible study to learn more about what I said I believed.

"You all are just a bunch of Jesus freaks, aren't you?" Henry said with a chuckle as we walked in one Sunday from church. Joseph was not with us, but Scotty really enjoyed the Sunday school.

"Look what I made!" Scotty handed Henry a colored page depicting a Bible story.

"Take that to your room," he answered, looking disinterested. I could see the resentment in his eyes as he sat slouched on the couch, flipping through the channels. He was upset at how much attention his dad gave this son that wasn't even his. Even more so, deep down, he resented himself for not being the best dad possible to his own son. Every other week was not enough for him, but he couldn't change the mistakes he had made in the past. I cared about my faith and following God, but with Henry's sour attitude about it, I quit going. I didn't stop believing in God; I just stopped showing it.

We started attending counseling, and the resentment only rose to the surface. The fire in his blood did not cool but worsened with each session.

"Would you consider Scotty living with your mother for a short time while the two of you work things out?" the counselor asked us. I was willing to try anything, especially since Henry even agreed to come to these sessions.

A week had passed, and I walked by Scotty's empty room while coming downstairs for breakfast. My heart clenched like a fist each time I thought about how quiet the house felt. I came into the kitchen and saw Henry preparing breakfast. He was whistling and humming some song while looking through the fridge for eggs. He turned back and saw me watching him and said, "Hey, honey, I made coffee." He had a huge grin on his face.

"How can you be so happy? I can't stand being without Scotty."

"You know what, Belle, you just need to let him go live with his dad so that we can be happy again. Everything will be just fine." I became dizzy, and I had to sit down as I listened to him say these things.

"I can't live without my son, but I really want our marriage to work. I think that perhaps we need to rethink things." I moved out a week later, and we continued to go to separate counseling sessions. The counselor requested to meet with Scotty, and I agreed. When I came to pick him up, the counselor informed me about the actions that she had just taken.

"We had no choice but to call CPS after everything Scotty told us," the counselor explained. I felt the shame and guilt overwhelm me when I received a call from CPS a few days later. The veil was slowly being lifted from my eyes, and I was beginning to realize that everything Scotty ever told me about Henry was true. I was allowed to take Scotty home because I was no longer living with Henry. I was not completely levelheaded yet because I still insisted that things could get better.

I stopped by every week to pick up Henry on the way

to Adam's hospital appointments. He never answered the door. I wrote him notes and left them in the mailbox on my way home, describing his son's health and everything that was going on. I thought it was important to keep him up to date on how to care for our son.

I continued to go to counseling even when Henry stopped. I learned that you didn't need to drink every day to be an alcoholic. I found out about the signs of abuse. Little by little, I was catching more glimpses of the reality that I was living.

Henry agreed to meet me at Kmart. I was sitting on a bench, waiting, when I saw him walk in. He had a tank top on and a huge red hickey on his chest. The dizzy feeling rushed through me, and it was then that it all snapped for me. Christina, my coworkers, my mom, Scotty and even Henry's own brother had all tried to warn me. Now that it was in front of my face, I could not deny the truth any longer. My marriage was over. I felt like the whole truth was laid out and revealed before me. That night I took my Bible out of the drawer and looked for verses on divorce. I wanted to know what God thought of divorce. I could feel myself coming undone.

Through my divorce, Marvin and his family surrounded me with help. Henry never did like me talking to any of my exes, even Scotty's dad, but now that it was all over, Marvin began helping me move into an apartment. His mother called me regularly and talked me through the heartache.

I became close friends with my neighbors in the

apartment complex. My birthday was coming up, and I really felt no desire to do anything now that Henry and I were not together.

"You need to get out," Abby insisted.

"I just don't know if I can handle this. Henry was supposed to take me out. Do you know that in all the years we were married, he never took me dancing once?"

"We'll take you dancing," Peter said. I gave them a funny look. I didn't want to, but at the same time, I did. I was finally beginning to accept the fact that my marriage was over.

We ended up having an amazing time that night. Some of us drank too much, but we made it home safe. Peter crashed on my couch, and I went upstairs to go to bed. I went into the closet and got out my box of wedding pictures. I clutched a photo to my chest and cried. I went downstairs and shook Peter awake. "Peter, will you hold me?" He didn't say a word; he just put his arms around me and let me sob into his chest.

Right away, Peter and I hit it off and began dating. Our sons got along nicely, and we really thought this could work. Scotty, Adam and I moved in with him and his son, and it looked like we could be a happy family.

☙☙☙

My old friend Cindy showed up out of the blue one day. At first I was a bit nervous because her husband dealt meth, and I had no desire to get back into that.

"You know, Dave and I completely changed our lives around. Actually, no, God changed our lives around. You should come with us to a service." Cindy had a huge smile across her face as she spoke.

A jolt of electricity ran through my blood as I tried to understand what I was hearing. This was the same woman who hooked me up with drugs, and here she was, inviting me to church. "I don't know about all that. I believe in God, but I don't know if church and religion are for me anymore." I thought about all the times Henry had criticized me about church.

"No, Belle, this is different. You should come check it out for yourself this Sunday because Dave is getting baptized."

"Are you kidding me? The Dave who used to sell drugs? You guys are hardcore bikers."

"Well, we've just been going to church and listening to God. Like I said, he changed our lives."

I agreed to go because deep down I wanted to and because I was curious to see what kind of place could change this couple so drastically. I went to Celebration Church for the first time, and I never regretted it. There were so many times before this that I had tried church out and seemed to fail. There were things in my life that I didn't want to give up. As the music started, I felt so calm and peaceful. I watched as people sang along and clapped. One woman in front of me really caught my attention. She was so into the music that she paid no mind to those around her. Her eyes were closed, she knew the lyrics by heart and her hands were raised in the air. She really looked like she was somewhere else in her mind. Watching her made me realize that I had never really done that. I had never really completely given myself over to God. To be honest, I could still feel myself holding back in that moment.

I answered the phone two weeks later, and Cindy was on the line. I was a bit annoyed because I knew she just wanted to invite me to church. The last experience was really nice, but I wasn't sure if I was ready to go back.

"You've got to come back to Celebration Church." I cringed a little inside. "We have a new pastor. You've got to come and listen to him teach." I could hear the excitement in her voice, but there was something else there, too: sincerity.

The second time I attended Celebration Church, I realized Cindy was sure right about one thing. This was not religion the way I'd known it before. Somehow when the music was playing or when the pastor was teaching, I could feel God right there with me. On top of all this, I could actually feel something inside of me slowly taking shape. My faith in God was blossoming, and I liked it. As I sat there in that service that day, I decided I was going to follow God. I looked at my life full of bad decisions up to that point, and I handed it all over to him. The pastor spoke about God's forgiveness, and that was what I wanted in my life.

And it didn't stop there. When I went home and had to deal with relationship issues with Peter or with Adam's diet, I would recall bits and pieces of what I was learning, and I could apply it to my life. I didn't need to be in church to pray — I could do it anywhere. I could pray for help or just out of thankfulness. I began to realize why people called it a relationship with Jesus and not just religion. Peter saw the change taking place in me and became curious as well.

"I think I want to go to church, too," he said while we were making dinner.

"Really?"

"Yeah, I see that it's helping you a lot, so I want to check it out."

When we arrived at church the next Sunday, I could tell he meant it. He wasn't just trying to tell me what I wanted to hear. I could see the same wonder on his face as he looked around at people singing. The sermon held his attention, and he followed the verses that showed on the big screens. Even though we were going to church, we continued to struggle with our issues.

As we attended church more, we learned more about the Bible. We learned that the way we were living was not God's way for us. Though Peter and I by then had been engaged for three years and lived together for five years, playing house just wasn't cutting it anymore. I always thought that since we were living together and we were intimate, it was almost like we were married. But we had separate finances and continued to live separate lives.

One day we met with our pastor and told him that we wanted to get married. He made sure we had pure intentions, and it was then that we decided not to sleep together for five months until our wedding. We couldn't change the past, but we could change our future. We felt like God wanted us to be obedient, and I believed he would bless our marriage because of it. I'd been so worried about having medical care for my son that fear of losing coverage if I married Peter almost caused me to miss out on the right way of living. For me, this marriage was in so many ways a step of faith. I had to trust that my son's medical needs would still be covered. So Peter and I got married.

As the years passed, I grew to know God more, and even though we attempted to do things the right way, our troubles never got easier. Peter wore his anger on his sleeve. He was well acquainted with the worst of curse words, which he dispensed regularly, but more than that, he hurled his unkind words on me. Sometimes his words hurt far worse than Henry's fists.

I was in the front yard one morning washing the walkway with the water hose. It was a nice sunny day, and Scotty's son, Jeremy, was playing on the porch. Scotty and his friend were sitting in the car in the driveway listening to music. It truly was a nice day to be outside. Jeremy threw one of his toys over the porch and laughed and giggled. Peter saw through the screen door and shouted at him, "Pick that up, Jeremy." Jeremy laughed and shook his head with another toy now in his hand.

"You better pick that up," Peter snapped.

"No," he said with a big smile.

"You are going to pick that up, or I am going to spank you."

"No, you are not going to spank him," Scotty shouted from the car.

"Yes, I am," he said with a mean laugh in his throat.

"No one is going to hit my son!" Scotty got out of the car as a string of curse words flowed from Peter's mouth. Scotty picked up Jeremy, strapped him into the car and left.

"Good riddance," Peter mumbled under his breath as we went back into the house.

Dealing with Peter's anger became harder and harder. My patience slowly melted away. Our marriage was becoming lukewarm, and I could hardly stand it. After everything we went through in growing closer to God, I just couldn't believe Peter was acting this way. My mom provided me with a place to stay while we tried to figure things out. Since she was an apartment manager, she let us stay in an empty apartment.

"Well, we can get everything all set up to make you feel at home."

"No, Mom. This is just temporary. Peter and I are going to try and work things out."

"If you say so, but you can stay as long as you need to."

The next morning, Scotty sat me down and very sternly said, "Look, Mom, Peter apologized to me, and I think he meant it. If you want to move back with him, that's fine. I only have 10 months left until I join the military. You have the rest of your life to deal with this."

I sat down at the table with my coffee mug thinking about what he just said. I waited for him to leave to call Peter.

"Look, Peter, I want to make things work, but things have got to change."

"Well, hello to you, too," was his reply.

"I'm being serious here."

"I know. I want this to work, too. I miss you guys. I apologized to Scotty, and I meant it."

"Yeah, Scotty told me about your apology. I can see you're trying, but it's just like this crazy cycle. You yell and scream, you apologize, we make up and then it happens again. Your anger erupts out of nowhere."

"I really want to change, I just have no idea how. I know we are going to church now, and it's been a big help in my life."

"Well, if you want to keep this relationship going, you're going to have to go to anger management classes." I was ready to argue and stand my ground, but his response shocked me.

"I will do anything. If some counselor can help me, then I will do it." We were both silent for a moment. I could tell he was waiting for my response, but I really had nothing to say.

"Please come back," he finally said. "I want you to stay at the house, and I will stay with a friend until we get this figured out." He showed up about an hour later to pick up all our stuff. We went home, and he packed a few bags and left.

Two weeks later, Peter showed up at the door unannounced.

"I've really got to talk to you." We hadn't spoken in several days, so it was nice to see him. I let him in and poured us some coffee while he sat down in the living room. I came and sat across from him and waited till he was ready to say whatever it was.

"Look, Belle, I've been talking to a pastor —"

"What about? Anger management classes?" I asked, cutting him off.

"This was better than that. I met with him not once, but twice. We talked for a long time, and he helped me get to the bottom of this anger. All I know is he prayed with me, and I asked God for forgiveness, and it just feels like everything is different now."

I could see that there was a difference in his face. His brow was no longer bent into a scowl, and each word came out of him with a sort of excitement. He moved back in that night, and we continued to go to church together. Right there in that moment, I was watching hundreds of answered prayers form. God was working in our lives and in our relationship. The more we prayed, attended church or just worked out our differences, the closer we got to God. He was moving to the center of our lives.

❧❧❧

I was so proud when Scotty joined the military. I visited him in Las Vegas during his first year of service. I was out for a jog, admiring the small houses with bright-green clipped lawns. The base was so similar to the one my family lived on when I was young. In between the blocks of cookie-cutter homes were parks with playgrounds. Memories of my youth were flowing through my mind as I jogged. As I turned a corner and ended up at a park, I completely stopped as I remembered a long-buried memory.

One day, a girl from my neighborhood and I went to the park. I noticed the McDarren brothers, boys I had seen on our block many times before.

At the playground, the boys coaxed us into a small green tunnel shaped like a turtle. They gently convinced us to remove our underpants. We were playing with "the choo-choo train," they said. At that time, I didn't have a full realization of what was going on, but the memory returned as I stood at the park horrified. My body began to shake as I held my hand over my mouth and wept.

Why is this memory returning now, Lord? I didn't understand why he was allowing this, but I asked for his help. I managed to pray and get myself back together and went home. When I returned to California, I managed to push the memory back into oblivion.

֎֎֎

Back in Fairfield, Peter and I decided to go to a prayer service one evening at Celebration Church. We were all standing in a circle at the front of the church, and Pastor

Vernon began preaching about forgiveness. I felt God trying to get my attention, as though he were tapping on my shoulder telling me to pay attention. *I have no enemies in this world. I have forgiven everyone,* I thought to myself. But then I felt God's tapping intensify, and the thought, *Forgive the McDarren boys,* came to mind. I had not uttered that name in my whole life, but I realized God was right. Pastor Vernon began to pray for all of us to forgive everyone in our lives, and tears were running down my face as I lifted my hands to God. I suddenly realized that someone had probably hurt those boys, too, and my crying became weeping. With each tear, I felt God washing the dark places.

God beckoned me further, and I looked at my friends standing in the circle and said, "I forgive the McDarren boys for molesting me." Although they didn't know what I was talking about, they supported me and prayed for me. In that moment, secret lines of shame written in my history were being erased. God was replacing it all with truth.

ৡৡৡ

Marvin's uncle died, and we felt the need to be there for him. Marvin and his wife, Janis, had built a strong relationship with us. Both of our spouses understood and respected the friendship that Marvin and I shared. As Marvin walked into the chapel, Peter mentioned, "Man, Scotty looks like him."

At that moment, I felt like something punched me in the stomach. I had never acknowledged the resemblance, but Peter was right. A seed of doubt was planted in my mind, and it began to tremble inside of me.

After the service, I walked up to Marvin to offer him my condolences, and it was like looking at his face for the first time. "I'm so sorry about your uncle, Marvin."

"Thank you. And thank you guys for being here. It means a lot to my family." I hugged him, and shortly after, I went home.

Peter could tell I was deeply troubled as we got ready for bed. "Belle, I'm really sorry about that comment I made about Scotty at the funeral. You know, I don't even know what I was thinking."

"No, don't be sorry. To be really honest with you, I am beginning to question things."

"What do you mean? Is there even grounds for this?"

"Oh, my goodness, Peter. I could take you through the whole story, but yes, there is. Fred cheated on me when we were young, and I did the exact same thing to him."

Peter sat down and wrapped his arms around me.

The next day, I called my same friend Karen and asked her, "Karen, did I love Fred so much that I just twisted things in my head to make him the father?"

"No. That's not it at all. Don't you remember the way we went over everything? Even after Scotty was two weeks late, we were so relieved. You really have nothing to worry about." Her words didn't console me at all.

Somehow, I knew this was something I had to resolve.

I knew that seed of doubt trembling inside of me was God's way of trying to reveal the truth. In October of that year, Marvin, Scotty and I took DNA tests. The results were going to take two weeks. Every day during that period, awful thoughts tormented my mind. It was like a terrible enemy beating his war drum at my doorstep.

What a whore you are — 26 years later, you still don't know who your child's father is? But as the thoughts came, God's voice was louder saying, "I am here. You have nothing to worry about. I am here."

I recalled the story from the Bible of the adulterous woman who Jesus let no one condemn. Another day, I would think, *What about my three grandsons? Are they going to have to change their last name? How could I ruin so many lives at once?*

But then God would whisper in my ear, "Do not worry, I am here." He would bring me the story of Meshach, Shadrach and Abednego, who were ordered to burn in the furnace for their faith in God. Then God himself went into the fire with them, and they came out untouched.

I was with my mother-in-law at a luncheon, and when my phone started ringing off the hook, I didn't answer because she knew nothing about it. I knew the results were in, so I hurried to drop my mother-in-law off and rushed home. I cancelled my plans for the evening, and I found myself at my favorite hiking trail. I climbed the steep trail, yelling at myself. I hated myself so much for making this huge mess. There was no more uncertainty. Marvin was

Scotty's father. The fact that Fred was never there for Scotty, but Marvin would have been, brought floods of regret. I sat at the top of the trail and looked out at the horizon. I just knew I had to call Scotty. When he answered, all I could do was apologize, over and over again. He accepted my apology and affirmed me. As I hung up the phone, a peace rushed over me. I suddenly realized I didn't hate myself, but that young, messed-up, hurt girl was really the focus of all my contempt. And I wasn't her anymore. I prayed to God and asked for his help.

I had to apologize to each person individually: Marvin, Scotty and even Fred. At the end of it all, I was so amazed at the answered prayers. Each person forgave me and was willing to move forward. Scotty knew Fred would always be his father, but he was able to welcome Marvin as a second dad and a grandfather to his children. When his wife got pregnant again, they named their son Ivan. What they didn't know was that was Marvin's middle name. In the end, I knew it was God's stamp of closure on the situation. Yet again, God was erasing lines of shame from my past and replacing them with the truth.

ক্তক্তক্ত

Before I knew it, I felt like God was asking me to volunteer at church. I started by welcoming new people to the church. Then I began teaching young boys Bible lessons on Wednesday night. I had come such a long way from that abused young girl, and I still had a long way to go. One Sunday, Pastor Smith brought all the teachers together for a meeting. He was encouraging us and making sure we were all doing all right.

"One thing I want you to know is you are all positive examples to these children. I need you all to be praying and making sure you are cleansing your life of any bad habits." I felt like my heart was snatched from my chest. Teaching these kids had become a part of me that I loved. But smoking was ingrained in me as well, and it was a part I didn't love so much. Each attempt to quit only made my desire to smoke stronger.

It had been a while since the meeting with Pastor Smith, and he had since left the church. I had quit and started smoking again too many times to count. I hadn't forgotten that conversation many years before. One day, I saw our associate pastor, Pastor Boon, as he was walking through the halls of the church. He wasn't at that first meeting, but I knew I could confide in him.

"Pastor Boon," I said with hesitation. "I need to step down from teaching. I am so sorry."

"What's going on? Is there something we can help with?" he asked.

"I have been trying to quit smoking for the past few years, and it is just impossible. I know, like you said last week, this is a bad example to the kids, and I just need to step down."

"Do you want to stop smoking?"

"Yes."

"Do you want to continue teaching?"

"Yes."

"Well, that's enough for me. You can continue," he said with a smile. It was like grace was written all over his face. Although I believed that I didn't deserve to keep teaching according to the standard set by Pastor Smith, Pastor Boon saw potential in me that I couldn't see in myself.

There were many instances at Celebration Church where I experienced grace like this. Pastor Vernon and his wife, Tina, asked me into their office in December of 2007 to discuss yet another duty they wanted me to help with at the church.

"We need someone we can trust, and you seem like the perfect fit." I had no words. Never in my life had I done such important work.

"This sounds like an amazing offer, but I really don't think I am qualified," I replied.

"We will train you on everything you need to know."

Now six years later, I am blessed to be trusted, loved and doing work that matters for my church.

I stand next to Peter as the band plays worship music. I love the way he closes his eyes and really talks to God. It inspires me to do the same. As Pastor Vernon walks up to the pulpit to start the day's sermon, I can't help but realize that I am that Disney princess living an amazing dream. It took many years of heartache and lots of hard work, but God's truth has been revealed in my life, and I am a new person.

THE PAST IS ONLY HISTORY
THE STORY OF ELIZABETH
WRITTEN BY LORI MCCLURE

Days of carefree living, of climbing trees and riding bikes halted after my uncle touched me. Maybe early signs of puberty that summer somehow sent a silent signal that I was different now. I didn't know. I only knew that my uncle turned into a different man. In turn, he changed me in a way that I could never undo.

Fear kept my mouth shut when he entered my bedroom under night's cover, and no matter how tight I squeezed my legs together, he found a way past my feeble defenses. I never spent another summer with my aunt and uncle, but at the age of 10, my innocence had ended and, with it, my childhood.

The contrast between my 9- and 10-year-old self shocked even me. Before, my life left room for little more than adventure and fun. I rode bikes to the quarry with my neighborhood friends, and my propensity toward tomboyish behavior kept me on a level playing field in sports with the boys. Hanging out with the guys was just easier. No sissy girl interruptions for minor injuries every five minutes needed. I relished their rough-and-tumble ways, and I fit right in. When I wasn't exploring, I delved into new worlds, reading every book I could get my hands on. Now, with the veil of childhood enchantment destroyed, a new progression began.

At the age of 11, boys became more than teammates, and I became Ted's secret girlfriend. Everyone at church loved charismatic 17-year-old Ted. He played the piano. He sang. He charmed. And he "dated" me privately because he knew no one would approve of our relationship.

The novelty and charm of my first real crush faded quickly. He controlled everything I did, including where I looked.

"What you lookin' at? I *said* what you *lookin'* at?" His fingers pressed hard into my face as he turned my head and held it firm.

"Nothin', Ted. Nothin'." If I looked anywhere but down, he believed irrational thoughts of his own making about my supposed lust and desire for other boys.

"Good." I tried not to jump as his fingers pinched my flesh as hard as they could. "You're not supposed to be looking at anything or anyone unless I give you permission." His intimidating laugh drifted through the air as I sat with a lingering sting on my skin. Pinches soon developed into hits and slaps. This was my first relationship with a boy, and Ted dominated everything about me before I even knew what happened.

Our secret relationship continued. Ted's sister often hung around with us, and one day I confided in her about what my uncle had done to me. She told Ted, who threatened to tell everyone in the church unless I confessed to my mother and father. Mortified by the thought of my friends knowing such dark secrets about me, I confided in my father.

In order to support the nine girls and two boys that made up our family, Dad worked two jobs. We steered clear of Mom, who ruled with an abusive hand against everyone. But Dad was sweet and kind. He tried, in what little time he had, to instill his Christian values in us. I didn't want to tell. I didn't want my daddy to know the ugly truth. Trapped by Ted's threats, I poured my shame out to Dad, and he set up a meeting with my aunt and uncle.

"I didn't do it," my uncle denied.

"I *know* he didn't do it." My aunt defended him.

"I'm sorry, Elizabeth, but I believe your uncle."

"Daddy!" His words knocked the wind right out of me, and an icy wind blew through my soul. My insides hardened, like stale bread left out on the kitchen counter, forgotten. "Fine." I stood up and walked out of the room. What more could I possibly say? Words felt useless.

After Ted learned the truth about my uncle, he became more aggressive with me. Until now, he'd only kissed me. Maybe he thought this news changed something.

On my 13th birthday, Ted and his sister came to pick me up for church, but instead of parking at church, he dropped his sister off. Once we were alone, he turned to me and said, "I have a birthday present for you," and drove us to a place in the mountains where teenagers went to make out. The sun faded, and under the starry night sky, he ordered me to get in the backseat. Things started as they normally did with a few kisses here and there, but then a switch flipped. Aggression and force and anger swirled together in a confusing, chaotic mess. Fear and panic swallowed me, and I spoke up to him for the first time. "Wait! What are you doing? No, Ted. No!"

My refusal only fueled his rage, and I felt the sting of his hand against my face, felt the unforgiving force of his bulky graduation ring against my cheek. Scared into silence, I stared at the dark blue interior and gave up the fight, while tears covered my face.

When the awful act ended, regret washed over Ted. He started crying and apologizing. I stared down at my bright yellow dress stained with blood. We were late for church, but I was in no shape to go with him now. As he drove me home, his apologies continued. "I'm sorry. I'm so sorry. Don't tell anyone, Elizabeth. You can't tell anyone." Before dropping me off, he gave me orders I obeyed.

"What happened?" my sister asked.

"I started my period." I gave my lines as instructed. While I stood in my house telling lies to my sister, Ted sat in church pretending his evil away.

༄༅༄༅

Our private relationship continued, which now included sex anywhere and anytime he wanted. His aggression continued. He towered over me, and he'd shake me like a ragdoll to "knock some sense into me," as he liked to say. But I didn't leave him, and unsurprisingly, I ended up pregnant a few months later. He denied any involvement with me, and his family called me wicked names, like slut and whore. The pastor even sided with charismatic, outgoing Ted. I felt worthlessness pool in the pit of my stomach like wet concrete.

Thankfully, my father believed me this time, and he sent me to a home for unwed mothers to spare me further shame. Rejection visited me at every turn. School kicked me out, and the church people were unkind. My circumstances left me alone, scared and feeling unloved.

The assumption of my parents, the assumption of everyone, ended with the hope of adoption. But I had no intention to give my baby boy away. After he was born, my father came to pick me up. I sat quiet, trying to work up the courage to speak. When we were a block from home, I said the words, "Daddy, I just want you to know that I'm going back tomorrow to get my son, Tom."

"Elizabeth, you can't. Once you sign the papers, it's over."

"I didn't sign them, Daddy." The words hung heavy between us, but I didn't care. No one would keep me from my baby boy!

The next day, I returned to pick up my son. Mom cried when I brought Tom home. My parents both fell in love with him immediately. My father helped me care for him and taught me how to be a mom. In the mess of all that had gone wrong, my son brought light and love into my life.

STRUCK

৵৵৵

At first, Ted told everyone he wanted to step in and marry me since I didn't know who the father was. That's what he said. But eventually he admitted that he was Tom's father. My parents urged me not to marry him, but Ted's power over me remained. I would go wherever he told me to go, do whatever he said to do. My own father didn't know what to do or how to help me.

I became Ted's wife at the age of 15. We left our church because of the scandal, but Ted's personality made it easy to find a new church and pastor who would marry us. He took me to a place where no one knew our past. He talked his way into a job at a new church. No one knew how old I was or what we'd been through, and we slipped right into a new life.

Privately the control and abuse intensified. Ted's jealousy manifested in him giving me bruises and bloody lips. My lies became habitual to cover the retribution of his anger that constantly showed on my face.

By the end of the year, I became pregnant with my second son, but even pregnancy provided no shield from his abuse. After one of my routine examinations, my doctor said, "Just wait here, Elizabeth. I'll be right back." I watched him walk out to the parking lot to where Ted sat in the car waiting.

"She's solid black and blue, and she's eight and a half months pregnant. Don't touch her again. If she ever comes in bruised up like this again, I'm calling the police." The doctor threatened him, so he never took me back.

Up until this point, my whole pregnancy had been full of bizarre happenings. The dichotomy between Ted's public and private lives bent my mind. Not only was he physically abusive but verbally as well. He constantly assaulted me with his words. "You're so stupid. You're retarded. You b****, you are *so* stupid." I believed every word. I believed I needed him to survive, that I was too mentally deficient to live alone.

He blamed his affairs on me as well. "The reason I'm unfaithful, Elizabeth, is because you don't satisfy me. You don't even know how to have sex." He was the only man I had ever been with, so I believed him. I thought, *Go ahead. Do what you need to do.* He convinced me he had a right to do whatever he wanted.

His erratic behavior continued. He began to steal from the churches he worked at, to rob small businesses and convenience stores. He manipulated a small group of teenage boys, all under the age of 16, convincing them to steal for him. His luck ran out when he stole a woman's purse right off her arm. He was found guilty, and instead of returning for his sentencing, he decided we would go on the run. During my pregnancy, he dragged us to Alaska, North Carolina, South Carolina, New Jersey and California. We stayed with anyone he could convince to let us in.

His behavior became sociopathic. He picked up hitchhikers, and just for sport, he'd slow down to drop them off. Then he'd press on the gas with one foot and kick them toward the door with the other, forcing them out of the moving vehicle. So much of what he did made little sense to me.

We moved from place to place because he stole from everyone everywhere we went. He stole heirloom jewelry from family members and friends; anything of value he took with no remorse. Guilt consumed me, but fear kept me silent. He used up every friend, family member or resource he had. At the end of his rope, he called his brother. "I don't know what I'm going to do. I don't have anywhere else to go."

"We can't give you any more money, Ted. You need to go turn yourself in. It's time. Look, you'll be out on parole in no time. Just turn yourself in."

We went back, and on the day I gave birth to my second son, Walter, Ted came to see me in the hospital and told me he was turning himself in, that things would get better. After he left, I wept. I felt alone. I couldn't understand why my life ended up this way. Why had I been given another son in the middle of such turmoil? Nothing made sense, but in the midst of my tears, I felt words rise up to offer comfort: *Your son is a gift from me.*

Indeed, Walter was a precious gift, and love for my boys continued to keep me sane through the confusion.

❧❧❧

THE PAST IS ONLY HISTORY

While Ted sat in prison, he made me live with his family. Ted's sister controlled me just as he did. She took my welfare checks and cashed them, using the money to pay bills and buy food. I had no say in anything. She wouldn't even allow me to breastfeed my baby. Walter was only 3 months old, but she made me switch him to formula. She became paranoid and jealous. She became consumed with the untrue idea that I was trying to take her husband away from her. Perhaps, to her twisted thinking, nursing was tempting him?

One day, her pastor came over, and they sat me down and told me I needed to leave. Embarrassed, I called my sister, who accepted me with open arms. Free from constant control, I found I could breathe easy. Every Sunday afternoon, I drove to Salem to see Ted in prison during visiting hours. At one of our visits, the chaplain led us into the chapel and said, "Ted has something he needs to share with you, Elizabeth, and then it will open the door for you to share anything you need to share with him."

"I have another child, Elizabeth." He told me the news nonchalantly about the other girl two years my junior. I looked at him with tears falling, but no words came. I only knew I wanted to end our relationship for good. I was done. Fear always kept me from leaving. Could I take care of a checkbook or figure out how to spend money or grocery shop? Ted had spent years highlighting my inadequacy.

The chaplain's words brought me back to reality. "Do you have anything you want to say to Ted, Elizabeth?"

"No." What did they expect me to say?

Ted spoke up. "Now is the time for you to come clean. You've forgiven me, and now I can forgive you if you tell me what you've been up to." He seemed convinced that I had been unfaithful, even though I hadn't.

"Nothing. I've been doing nothing."

Shock kept my words few. The bell rang signaling the end of our visitation, and the chaplain took the long walk with me to my car. He saw the silent tears roll down my face and said, "Don't do anything rash. He's really a changed man. He's going to be paroled in just a short time, and he's going to need your help. Can I tell Ted you'll help him?"

"Yeah," I said with no feeling. "I don't want him to sit in prison forever. I can help."

"Don't do anything rash, Elizabeth." The chaplain left me with his final charge. Why was I the one being instructed to keep myself from rash behavior?

As I recounted the events of my visit to my sister, I saw her anger rise.

In my mind, everything shut off, and I began to imagine a life without Ted. I nervously approached my father to tell him my plans. "Daddy, I'm divorcing Ted."

"It's about time. You know how I feel about divorce, but, Elizabeth, you cannot live like this forever. You deserve more." Relief washed over me, and for the first time, I believed I could live without Ted.

"You can do this, Elizabeth," my sister encouraged me. I started taking care of my own money and learning how to manage my own life. I put Ted out of my mind. I even went to a party at my sister Alice's house. My sister Mary came with her boyfriend who brought his friend Oliver. All night Oliver stood across the room staring at me. When our eyes met, he looked down.

For the first time in my life, I approached a boy to speak to him. "I'm not a very good dancer, but do you wanna dance with me?"

Our hands locked, and as we danced our eyes met. His cute and smiling dimpled face oozed gentleness. "You are so beautiful," he said as my insides melted with the sincerity of his words. I liked Oliver, not just because he was handsome, but because he was peaceful and kind in the way he spoke to others, in the way he treated me.

All night we danced with only each other. The music played while our feet kept time, and as I looked up at him, he reached down and pressed his lips to mine. The connection I felt to him surprised me. A strong force drew me to him, and our bond seemed special.

Night turned to early morning, and as the partygoers scattered, Mary and her boyfriend said, "Why don't we go out for a drive?" The four of us piled into the car, Oliver and I in the backseat. We sat and talked.

Mary and her boyfriend fell asleep in the front seat, and Oliver said, "Let's take a walk." We wandered and talked until daylight, and he overwhelmed me with his kindness. After that night, he called and came around every few days, and I knew what I needed to do.

I went to visit Ted, who was still in prison, and told

him I wanted a divorce. He fumed, and rage flashed in his eyes. His hands pounded the table with too much force, and the guards came and removed him from the room. I didn't realize what I had started.

Soon Ted's brother came to see me, but I stood my ground. "I'm filing for divorce, and no one can stop me." He finally left, and I had somewhere to be, so my father kept the boys for me. When I got back, my boys were gone. Dad said Ted's family told him I'd given my permission for the boys to spend the night. Panic welled up within me. His family had kidnapped my boys, and I had no idea how to find them.

Frantic, I rushed to Ted's brother's house to find my boys, but he wouldn't help me. Overwhelmed, my fear turned to anger as I fought with him, pleading to know where my boys were. My hands formed into fists as he refused to tell me any information, and I pounded him with flailing punches. Our fight continued as my fragile emotions exploded in violent actions. Lost and out of control, I feared I would never see my boys again.

Eventually the fighting stopped, and he told me the terms I must agree to. I needed to stop the divorce and help Ted get paroled. I agreed out of desperation. The next day Ted came over from the halfway house I'd already helped him get into. He raped me to prove his ownership of me still stood strong. Then his family returned with my boys. Once they were back in my arms, I knew I would never let them go.

A few months later, I was pregnant and horrified. I

had been intimate with Oliver, and I had been raped by Ted. I panicked and decided on abortion as my answer. I secretly went to a doctor who began the process of a seaweed abortion and sent me home for the night. I returned the next day weeping, begging them to stop the process, but nothing could be done. It was too late into the procedure, and my insides were already dried up. Removing the baby had to come next, and sorrow like I'd never known consumed me. Over and over, the only thought to echo through my mind was, *What have I done?*

෧෧෧

Ted showed up one day to take me and the boys on a drive to the river. I felt I had no choice but to go. I feared I could lose my boys if I angered him. I didn't trust Ted or his family. I knew they were capable of anything.

Ted still lived at the halfway house, so he came to pick us up from my parents' house where we were living. The frigid air chilled me less than Ted's presence. His behavior scared me as we got closer to the river. He seethed with anger as he drove and muttered over and over, "I could just kill you for all you've done to me. I could just kill you." Fear caught in my throat as I looked back to check on the boys in the backseat.

He pulled the car up next to the water and turned to me. "Get out of the car. Now!" I jumped and reached for the door handle as he made his way out of the driver's side.

Grab the keys, Elizabeth. The thought came, and I turned one last time to snatch the keys and shove them in my pocket. "I'll be right back, boys. Mommy loves you."

I shut the passenger door, and my heart broke as I heard 3-year-old Tom's muffled screams. He stood in the backseat, leaned against the window watching me and yelling, "Mommy! Mommy!"

My stomach knotted as I tried to think of a way out, but Ted clutched my arm and marched me farther into the woods as he spewed more threatening words. "I could just kill you. I could just kill you. I could just kill you." His crazed repetition echoed through the air, and then he stopped, looked me in the eye and said, "I *will* kill you."

His 6-foot, 1-inch frame towered over my 5-foot body, and his hands reached out and surrounded my throat in a vice-like grip. The world faded, and I collapsed. Ted reached down and picked my floppy body up, threw me into the chilly river and walked away. Startled back to consciousness by the frosty waters, thoughts of my boys consumed me. *I'm dying. I'm dying, and there's nobody to care for my babies.* I prayed a desperate prayer. *Jesus, please take care of my boys.* I could feel myself drifting away until Ted returned to fish me out of the water. He needed the keys I had shoved in my pocket. His anger turned to regret as he got me in the car. I sat soaking wet, freezing and aching to be far, far away from this monster of a man.

"I'm sorry, Elizabeth. I'm so sorry."

"If you're really sorry, Ted, then take me back to Mom

and Daddy's house." The hoarseness of my voice made the words barely audible. I sat frozen from the inside out, and when we reached home, his apologetic nature disappeared as he gave a final warning.

"If you ever tell *anyone* what happened, I'll come back and finish you off. If you ever tell … if you *ever* tell …" His eyes were desperate and evil, and I rushed to get inside with the boys, hurrying to distance us as far away from this crazy man as I could.

"What's wrong?" Mary looked at my sopping wet sweatshirt and jeans, saw the marks around my neck and the abrasions on my face. I looked like I'd been in a fight, a one-sided fight though it was, and weariness wracked my body. I went to answer Mary, but the words wouldn't come. He had strangled the voice right out of me, but Mary could see the evidence all over me, and no explanation was needed.

A few hours later, Ted returned in his jeans and zip-up windbreaker, the one with the elastic-gathered poofy waist that I hated. He lunged toward me, and Mary jumped on his back and pummeled him over and over as hard as she could. Ted threw her to the ground and lifted his hand, bringing it down hard across her face. Everything happened so fast, and Mary grabbed a broom handle and threw all her force behind it, smashing it against Ted's body again and again until he fled.

My sister Mary had whooped Ted, and right or wrong, we were both filled with more than enough satisfaction knowing he'd just been beaten by a girl.

STRUCK

Before long, Ted returned to stealing. Desperate to get out of town, he showed up with an offer. "I'll get out of your life forever, Elizabeth, if you'll give me your welfare check. I've got to get out of town, and I have no money. Give it to me, and you'll never see me again." There was nothing to think about. I gave him the paltry $210. He took it and left town.

৵৵৵

When I became involved with Oliver romantically, I warned him that I'd never marry again. We eventually moved in together. My mindset went to the opposite extreme from my relationship with Ted. If Oliver ever hinted that I *had* to do anything, I told him, "You *never* tell me what to do, ever. Don't ever, *ever* tell me to do anything." Determined never to let a man hurt me again, I made my opinions clear. Somehow, Oliver's patience never wore out.

When he still asked me to marry him, I said, "No, I'm never going to marry again. I won't allow another man to be my boss." I wouldn't allow myself to be under the subjection of another man or live in total and complete obedience to another human being. I told him, "I do not love you. I do not think I will ever be able to love another man. I just cannot love you, Oliver."

Distressed about our living situation, he felt torn because his parents were pastors. Even though he wasn't a

Christian, he wanted to end the stress he caused his parents. "Elizabeth, I can't stay living with you because I wasn't raised like this. Please marry me."

My boys loved him so much because he fathered them with peace and provided a safe home for all of us. He never yelled or jerked them around like Ted had. His calm, gentle, loving ways soaked all our weary and wounded hearts. Even when I told him I didn't love him, that I wasn't sure I could ever love him, he said, "I love you enough for the both of us."

I finally agreed to marry Oliver, but the idea still scared me. On our wedding day, I stood in the back of the church with my dad, crying in my lime-green dress decorated with daisies on the puffy sleeves and hem. "Daddy, I'm so afraid. I'm so afraid to belong to someone again."

"Let me pray for you, Elizabeth." The words of his reassuring prayer washed over me, and we turned the corner to walk down the aisle.

"You know, if he's mean to me, I'll leave him. I won't stay. I don't know what it will do to our boys if this doesn't work because they love him so much." A new wave of anxiety welled within me.

"It's going to be okay, Elizabeth. Everything's going to be okay." My fingers gripped the simple daisy bouquet, and my veil gently flowed over my long hair as I took a deep breath and steadied myself.

Tears still falling, I looked down the aisle to see sweet Oliver in his apple-green suit. His excitement eased my nerves, and his eyes spoke to me as I walked toward him, as if to say over and over to the rhythm of my beating heart, *You can trust me, you can trust me, you can trust me.* Somehow this man truly loved me. Somehow he was in awe of me. Despite all I had been through, he found a way to love me, even in my brokenness. He knew all about my past, and his love and reassurance never failed. It seemed impossible. The whole day brought one precious memory after the next.

Life with Oliver far exceeded my expectations, but I still carried the shame of my past with me. We married at age 18 and 19. Not long after, I became pregnant with another son, Jesse. Happiness started replacing pain, but guilt kept me bound through memories and small reminders. Through the years, people always tried to figure out how long we'd been together when they saw the age of my boys. They had no idea I'd already lived a lifetime of pain and heartache with another man, and I had no intention of disclosing my past.

They'd say, "So how long have you two been married? Four or five years?"

"Oh, we've been married a little while." I tried to evade the questions.

"Really … how long have you been married?"

"Look, I'm not gonna go there. It doesn't matter, anyway. You just want to find out how old I am and if we lived together before we were married. I'm young, and yes, we did!" My divorce and past chained embarrassment to me that I couldn't break free from.

But our lives were happy, filled with gentleness and laughter. We had a good life with friends and family. Dad wanted me in church, and he often reminded me of how much God loved me when he picked up the boys for church. I had no desire to go, and I looked forward to the extra sleep I gained on Sunday mornings. Besides, I'd come to the conclusion that God wasn't real. How could he be real after all I'd been through? It seemed impossible after all the pain and suffering I'd endured.

One night, I went to bed as usual. Thoughts of God were far away. On November 23, I woke up wide-awake in the middle of the night, and I heard a voice as clear as my own say, "You've got to get your life in order. In three months, I will take your life."

The fire I felt inside my body when I heard the voice overwhelmed me, and I needed no convincing. Without question, I knew the voice belonged to God deep inside of me, like hearing my own father or mother's voice. I just knew. The power of God's presence overshadowed me and reached far beyond any experience I ever had. No words adequately described the persuasive power of his voice. I couldn't deny God any longer. He had spoken to me, and I had no desire to refuse him. I wanted him. With tears falling down my face, I woke Oliver and told him I wanted to give my heart to God. I wanted our lives to be different, for the boys to know God. We prayed and cried, and I determined to be a Christian like my father.

We went to church the following Sunday, and I walked up to the altar at the end of the service as a public declaration of my new belief in God. I'd already given my heart to the Lord. I knew he had changed me forever. I knew everything would be different. I knew we could no longer live the way we were living. I needed to get every bit of God in front of my children in the three months that I had left. The words rang in my head, constantly reminding me I had three months to get my life in order, and my children needed to hear about God. I was certain my life would soon end.

Oliver and I didn't come to the Lord because our lives were horribly bad. We had a good life filled with laughter and love. I came to the Lord because he spoke to me, and I couldn't deny the voice of the Lord when I heard it. I knew I had a choice, but I didn't want another one. And so my journey with God began. I told the pastor and his wife about the voice I'd heard, and they encouraged me not to tell anyone. They said no one would believe me. They said, "Why would God speak to you?"

"I don't know why God would speak to me, but he did." I didn't care that no one believed me. I went to church the next three months, read my Bible feverishly and talked to my boys about how much Jesus loved them. I took notes on every sermon and explained the messages to my children after each service. I wanted them to know Jesus, no matter what happened to me.

Convinced my death neared closer with every passing day, a pleading prayer escaped my lips. "I will serve you forever, God, if you let me live. I want to be the one to raise my children and teach them about you." My heart ached at the thought of leaving them. I couldn't bear all the unknown questions.

February 23 came. As the day neared its end, Oliver and I sat in our van on the freeway, headed home. We reached toward one another and locked hands. "The day's almost over. It's all going to be okay." We both felt relief that we'd made it through the day.

We were almost to our exit when it happened. A man driving behind us fell asleep at the wheel. He hit us, and our car flew over two trees and spun around several times before landing in a ditch in a nearby field. The other man's car ran up a telephone pole.

I looked at Oliver. I looked at Walter in the backseat. I looked down at myself. We were all okay. I heard the voice again. "Just like this, I can take your life." God answered my prayer and let me live. Even the man who hit us walked away unharmed from the accident.

The accident further inspired me to tell others about Jesus' love. I volunteered to be the bus captain to pick up children for church. I spent hours knocking on doors and inviting people to come. I started picking up just a few children, and soon my bus filled up every week. It thrilled me to bring them all to church so they could learn more about the wonderful love of God. My insides lit up with enthusiasm for all things related to God.

Oliver and I grew quickly in our faith. We started teaching and helping in any way we could. And throughout our time in ministering to others, God slowly changed me as he brought issues to my mind and heart to deal with. Trusting others presented a challenge for me, and wounds from all the abuse I endured still lingered.

God gently dealt with me about every matter that plagued me. I had repressed so many hurts, but God began to bring each one up as I could deal with it. We were in a service one night, and the minister said, "There are people here who have bitterness in their heart." I began to weep as memories flooded back to me. I prayed at the front of the church for hours, and I wept and wept and asked God to take it all from me.

When I got up from the altar, it wasn't over. I began to read every single book I could find about emotional health and how to recover from abuse and rape. I had avoided all of it, but now the time for mending had come. Slowly, God continued to deal with me. Memories came back, and I cried and prayed until the hurt faded. I would be okay for an hour or a day before a new surge of pain came. Again, I would cry and pray, and Oliver would pray with me. Soon the time between tears and pain stretched into weeks and months. I grew stronger as the broken places inside me filled with God's love.

God led us to people who suffered as I had suffered. We worked with people in abusive situations. I worked at the battered women's shelter, talking to women contemplating abortion, women who had already had abortions. The challenge of talking about my past brought memories back, and the weight of what I'd done ate away at me; the weight of killing my own baby became too great to bear.

THE PAST IS ONLY HISTORY

I stopped working at the women's shelter. I became depressed. We even left the ministry we'd been at for 12 years because my depression kept me from going to church. We didn't know what was wrong. I felt ashamed, but I had no choice. I could no longer function anymore.

We packed up and came to Celebration Church in a motor home. When we arrived they were in the middle of a time of 40 days of prayer and fasting. I went every single night as they met for prayer, and every night God continued the process of growth he'd begun so long ago. I went to the doctor and was given antidepressants, and I continued praying. I stopped fearing other people as God loved me through the people of Celebration Church. They were a group of people who loved fiercely because they had been fiercely loved. They had all weathered their own storms, and they believed in God's changing power because they'd experienced it in their own lives. In the safety of a loving community, I became whole.

As a young girl, I had been dismissed and looked down upon by the churches I'd been a part of. I had needed protection, and it hadn't come. Now to be a part of a church fueled only by the desire to love, I couldn't help but remember the hurt of my childhood. But God cared enough to bring me to a group of people willing and ready to love me through the dark times I faced, and gratitude swelled within me.

I had so much inadequacy built up inside for not having finished school, for my divorce, for the abuse, for the abortion — all of it had left me fearful, ashamed and untrusting of others. Even though I had forgiven Ted and my uncle and even my father for not protecting me, somehow I had the most trouble forgiving myself. Once forgiveness came, the tormenting memories faded. The guilt left. The reality of my past remained, but the condemnation disappeared. And even though the reality of my past remained, I could see it as just a part of my history instead of a burden of shame to hide.

Oliver gently held me and prayed with me as he encouraged me. "God forgives you, honey. He's forgiven you." I dwelled on the forgiveness and love of God for me. I believed there was nothing God couldn't forgive, and slowly the chains that held me tight for so many years began to unlock and drop around me.

Soon I began to tell my story to others without fear and shame. I could share how God desired to make us new, to forgive and love and how there was no way to earn any of it. I could never do enough good to earn the mercy of God. It just comes as a gift for all of us. And his forgiveness just comes. I can't go back and fix anything. I can't do enough things to make any of it right. I can't apologize enough or do enough good deeds. None of that was necessary. In spite of every mistake I'd made, the mercy and grace of God is far bigger than my shame. No matter how many things I wished I could undo, I learned to believe God's love would always be bigger and stronger than my past. After all, the past is only history.

HOME FOR GOOD
THE STORY OF RICH
WRITTEN BY KAREN KOCZWARA

Whack. Whack.

The belt flew across my skin, and I braced myself for the painful sting.

Just take it, kid. There's no use in fighting back.

The stench of beer and cigarettes closed in on me, and I tried not to gag beneath my father's breath.

Please, just stop it. Just stop right now!

I wanted to cry, wanted to let the tears come in a torrent. But I held them back, trying to be brave.

Suck it up, kid. The old man's drunk. You know the drill. Just suck it up, and go to sleep. Maybe things will be better tomorrow.

But even as I tried to convince myself, I knew the truth. Tomorrow would not be better. Nor the day after.

There would be more bruises, more curse words, more drunken rages.

Someday, perhaps, I'd escape from this madness for good. And when I did, I would never look back.

❧❧❧

I was born in 1975 in Northern California to a Native American mother and a Caucasian father. When I was just

5 years old, my parents divorced. At an age when most little boys' biggest decisions revolve around which toy car to play with, I was forced to make a decision that would change the rest of my life.

"Do you want to live with your mom or your dad?" the judge asked me.

I chose my father.

My mother did not fight for me. She had her hands full with four other children from a previous marriage. We went our separate ways, and I followed my father out those courtroom doors. I would not see my mother again for years.

My father and I moved out and began a life of our own. He dabbled with work in the construction industry, never able to hold down a job for long.

We moved from place to place, bunking with friends and renting rooms from folks who advertised in the newspaper. The little bit of stability I'd experienced early on vanished in the wake of the divorce.

I started school, not sure if I'd be able to finish out the year with my new friends. Home soon became a distant memory.

When I was 6 years old, my father began drinking more heavily. One Friday night, I finished up my homework and headed off to bed. As I tossed and turned, trying to fall asleep, my father wandered into the room and climbed into the bed we shared. The stench of alcohol was strong on his breath, and I tried to scoot away from him.

"Stop moving, kid! What are you doing? What's your f***ing problem?!" he screamed.

Frightened of his booming voice, I huddled under the covers and began to cry. *Why is Dad being so mean? What did I do to make him so mad?*

"Get outta here!" My father kicked me out of the bed, and I tumbled to the ground. He clenched his fists and began punching me, one hit after another. I braced myself beneath the beating, tears streaming down my face in the dark.

"Don't move, kid!" My father now hovered inches away, a shadow of an angry monster as he continued whipping me.

I tried to be brave, tried to hold it together beneath his wrath, for I sensed it would only anger him more if I didn't. My skin smarted, and I suspected there would be blood or at least a bruise. At last, unable to sustain any more, I collapsed on the floor and blacked out.

The beating was just the beginning of my father's abuse. He began regularly frequenting bars, often stumbling home well past midnight with beer on his breath. In his drunken rage, he beat me until he was satisfied and then rolled over and went to sleep. In the morning, he went on his way, while I avoided his eyes and covered my bruises, filled with shame and fear.

We often visited my father's relatives, who lived nearby. One day, we headed over to my grandmother's sister's house. The old woman's place, filled with breakable antiques and expensive furniture, was not especially suitable for an active young boy. My cousin and I began playing with an old glass vase, and in our carelessness, it broke.

"You are gonna get a whoopin', huh?" My cousin stared up at me, wide-eyed with horror.

My stomach tightened as I surveyed the shattered pieces at our feet. My cousin had seen my father's angry streak and knew what he was capable of. I cringed, knowing I had it coming. There was no getting out of this one.

When my father returned from the liquor store, he flew into a rage. "Come here, kid! You break that vase? You think that's funny? Well, I got somethin' for you!" He whipped off his belt and began chasing me around the room, cursing and screaming. I ducked and ran for my life, trying to avoid yet another lashing. My relatives stood nearby, laughing as though it was some sort of lighthearted playground game.

As I flew into the kitchen, my grandmother grabbed me and held me back. She then looked me square in the eye, hers filled with a terror I'd never seen before. "Just get it over with, son," she whispered.

My father pushed me on the ground and began whipping me in front of everyone. I closed my eyes and tried to block it out. His voice grew louder and angrier as the curse words flew out one on top of the other. Shame seeped in, and I fought to keep from crying. After 10 minutes of torture, my father finally released me and ordered me to go sit on the couch.

I trudged into the living room, my legs shaking as I stumbled to the couch. I then hung my head and waited for whatever was to come next. *Just get it over with, and stop humiliating me. Just leave me alone!*

"Hey, now, that wasn't right," one of my relatives said to my father.

"Look here. When it's your kid, you do what you want. Got it?" my father snapped.

"Now, now, I know you are a single father and under a lot of stress. Just take it easy on the boy," my grandmother interjected.

I lifted my head and stared at them, a bunch of gawkers who'd just seen the show of a lifetime. *Well, is that it? Aren't you going to stand up for me? Do something more? Take my father down?* I waited, but no one else said a word. They were too afraid of him, too knee-deep in their own set of problems. That horrible day, a piece of me gave up on humanity. *I thought grownups were supposed to be good, but maybe they're not. If they won't fight for me, I'll just have to learn to fight for myself.*

We spent the next few years moving from place to place, never staying in one area long. When we could not afford to pay rent, we slept in my father's little Ford Pinto at rest stops and used the facilities there. We often stayed in shelters in the darkest places of Oakland, surrounded by strange, dirty men and drug dealers.

I shifted uncomfortably on my tiny cot and tried to fall asleep next to my father, but out of the corner of my eye, I spotted a guy staring at me. I didn't know everything these guys were capable of, but I feared what they might want to do to a little kid like me. I said a silent prayer, hoping that morning would come fast so we could get back on the road.

My father continued hitting the bars, drinking and meeting up with new women. One evening, he brought me along with him on a date to the drive-in movie. As the flick started, my father moved closer to his date, and they began making out in the front seat. Disgusted, I tried to scoot out of the way, but they kept up the kissing and groping. *Gross, Dad! Did you forget I'm right here? I'm just a kid!*

I moved from school to school, finding it difficult to make friends because I never stayed long. Just when I thought I'd finally settled in, my father whisked us away in the middle of the night, and I never returned again. My father had never graduated from high school and did not consider education a priority. He didn't help me with my homework, but I tried to figure everything out the best I could. Somehow, I always passed my classes.

I heard my peers discuss sports, weekend sleepovers and new toys, and I wondered what that must be like. I'd never gotten a new toy in my life, much less had a sleepover or joined any sports teams. I felt like an outsider always looking in, dreaming about a life I was not sure I'd ever have. *Why can't I just be normal?* I wondered sadly.

When my father could find work, he often pulled me out of school and took me with him. While living in the Bay Area, he made friends with a guy in the construction industry, and the guy paid him under the table to do part-time work at a lumber yard. One day, I sat in the car for more than six hours in the scorching heat while he worked nearby. While other kids played video games, kicked the soccer ball around and built Lego creations, I amused myself by throwing rocks and hitting things with sticks. It was the only way to pass the long, boring days.

The beatings continued. Though my father never gave me a chance to complete a full year of school, he grew angry when I brought home D's and F's. "Are you stupid, boy? You can't be gettin' grades like this!" He chased after me, smacking me repeatedly, his eyes fiery with rage. I could smell the stench of cigarette smoke on his clothes, and it stung my eyes. I wanted to fight back, but I knew better. I was just a kid, a victim without a voice. Speaking up would only make things worse.

My father got food stamps from the government, and we lived off of them. When the food stamps first arrived each month, he came home with a big steak for dinner, topping the meal off with a pot of Rice-A-Roni. Once in a while, we dined on McDonald's hamburgers. I always stuffed the food down quickly, knowing there might be nothing to eat the next day. Sure enough, following the steak dinner, my stomach grumbled for days.

"What's for dinner?" I asked my father when I got back from school.

He shrugged. "Nothin' left, kid. Sorry."

I went to bed with an empty belly, dreaming about that steak dinner.

STRUCK

I spent the rest of my elementary school years living between shelters, rundown apartments and rest stops all over Northern California. One night, my father pulled the Pinto into a rest stop parking lot and climbed out to light a cigarette. I curled up my legs on the dirty car seat and stared down at my tattered hand-me-down pants. As I glanced back up, I caught the moon just peeking out in the night sky. *Is this it?* I wondered with despair. *My life sucks. I don't want to live like this. Surely, there must be more out there.*

My grandmother's house remained my only reprieve in the midst of the poverty and chaos. My grandmother took me school shopping at Kmart every year. Though the clothes were not high fashion, they were a far cry from the worn-out duds I wore the rest of the year. I watched with wide-eyed envy as my cousin piled up the goods at his house — GI Joe, Transformers and He-Man action figures and high-top Air Jordan tennis shoes. *What must it be like to get new toys all the time?* I mused. *What must it be like to sleep in the same bed every night, to eat three hearty meals a day, to go to the same school all year long?*

One day, I overheard my father begging my grandmother for money. "Please. I need it for the kid," he whined. "Can you spare a few bucks?"

I heard my grandmother sigh. "I will this time, but you've got to get yourself a stable job. I can't keep throwing money your way," she snapped impatiently. "And don't you count on getting a dime of it when I'm gone someday."

HOME FOR GOOD

My father drifted in and out of odd jobs, always scrounging up just enough cash to put some gas in the car. When I was 11, we secured an apartment, and for the first time in my life, I had my own room. One day, I wandered into my father's room and discovered a stash of magazines scattered around his bed. Scantily clad women in lingerie and red lipstick smiled at me from the covers. Curious, I picked up the magazines and flipped through, my eyes bulging at the glossy photos inside. *Whoa. So this is what my dad's doing in here.*

I'd known my father was obsessed with women, and I'd seen him bring home a few from the local bar. But this was a whole new world I was not aware of. I found myself unable to turn away from the pages. I had not grown up with a mother and did not know how to treat women. *Perhaps all guys look at this kind of stuff,* I reasoned.

Next, I discovered my father's pornographic videos. More than once, I walked in to see him checking out the naked couples on TV. Again, my curiosity was roused. As a preadolescent boy with a set of raging hormones, I could not look away. From then on, I developed my own addiction, sneaking the magazines into my own bed and watching the videos with my father. He did not discourage me, as he was sucked in as well. His secret lifestyle became my secret lifestyle for the next five years.

One afternoon, while in the kitchen, my father made a sneering remark. As he pulled off his belt to whip me, I quickly glanced at the steak knife on the counter. *I could hurt him with this,* I thought, a little thrill running up my spine. A sense of courage welled up in me, and I grabbed the knife and waved it in my father's face. "If you hit me, I will stab you right now!" I screamed, surprised at the strength of my own voice.

"You wouldn't dare!" My father charged at me with the belt, and I chased after him wielding the knife. Several minutes later, the next-door neighbor charged through the front door.

"Put the knife down!" she cried frantically.

Suddenly, the cops burst through the front door. "What's going on in here? We got a call that there's been screaming and yelling. Is everything okay?"

I set the knife down and shook my head. "Everything is fine here," I lied, my heart thumping so loud in my chest I was sure everyone in the room could hear.

My father stared at me from across the kitchen, his eyes steely and wary, as though to say, "Don't you dare. Don't you dare tell them, kid."

The police went on their way, and the neighbor followed them out. I stormed off to bed, too upset to face my father again. *Why, Rich? That was your big chance. The cops came out to protect you, and you didn't tell them what your father did to you! You should have spoken up!* I was glad the neighbor had called and knew I should have reported the abuse. I was 12 years old now, nearly a teenager. My father could not pin me down forever. Soon, I'd gain enough strength to take him down. *You're lucky, Dad. You got off the hook this time, but watch out. I'm ready to fight back now.*

HOME FOR GOOD

From that day on, I made up my mind that my father would never hit me again. I had endured six years of physical abuse, on top of emotional and physical neglect, and I'd had enough. My father had never once sat down with me to impart a word of wisdom, never once told me he was proud of me or that he loved me. He had dragged me around for too long, and I was sick of it. I would find a way to escape this madness someday, hopefully sooner than later.

My father looked at me differently from then on, and the beatings stopped. But he kept up his gypsy lifestyle, moving from job to job and place to place. The lifestyle of smoking, drinking, sex and poverty continued, and I tried my best to stay out of his way. I developed my own sex addiction, unable to stop looking at porn. Deep down, I felt shame as I hid my terrible secret from the world.

I started classes at yet another school in a new town, and there, I met a new friend. One day, he invited me to church down the street. I had never been to church in my life and had no idea what to expect. But it sounded like a nice thing to do on a Sunday morning and would certainly be an escape from the dingy, smoke-filled apartment I shared with my father.

"Sure, I'll go," I agreed.

On the way, I asked him what we'd do once we arrived.

"It's cool. They start off with a time of worship, singing songs and stuff. Then the pastor shares, and then there's usually a prayer time at the end."

"Huh." That was all new to me. But I was up for checking it out.

We walked through the doors and took a seat in the back pew. Just as my friend had said, a group of singers stood onstage with instruments, singing along with the folks in the pews. I glanced around and noticed a pretty girl saunter in.

"Who's that?" I whispered, nudging my friend.

"Oh, that's Laura. She goes to the youth group here."

The pastor began speaking, and I leaned in with interest, wondering what he had to say. He read out of a Bible and talked about God. *This is kinda cool,* I thought to myself. I didn't know much about God, but in a way, I'd always believed in him. My mind drifted to the night I'd stared up at the moon in the rest stop parking lot. I was so sure there was something bigger out there, something beyond my crummy little world. Now, sitting here, I wondered if this church stuff might be a part of that something bigger.

The following week, I decided to check out the youth group. A bunch of kids my age milled together, listening as the youth pastor shared a heartfelt message.

"We all go through struggles in life. Some of us face struggles so difficult that we wonder how we'll ever find our way out," he began. "Well, you should know that there is someone out there who does not want you to have victory. His name is Satan, and he is a real enemy. He is doing everything in his power to defeat you. But there's good news. God sent his son, Jesus, to earth to die for the wrong things we've done so that we could experience that victory. If you're sitting here today wondering if you've messed up too badly for God to forgive you, be assured that you have not. There is nothing you can do that will keep God from pursuing you. He loves you that much. If you have not given your heart to him, you can pray today and invite him to be a part of your life. You don't have to wait a day longer."

Whoa. Something inside of me clicked, and I leaned in further to listen. *Victory. I want to experience that. But I can't even imagine what that feels like, because I've spent so long being oppressed. Is it possible that there is a God out there who really cares about a kid like me?*

After the message, the pastor gave an altar call, inviting anyone who wanted to pray to invite Jesus into his or her life to come forward. I did not go forward, but I closed my eyes and let the words penetrate my heart. *God, I want that. I want what this pastor is talking about. I want victory from this enemy so that I can live a free life. Would you please forgive me and come into my heart? I want victory in you. Starting right now.*

Tears streamed down my face as I opened my eyes. I felt as if a weight I'd been carrying around my entire life had disappeared. I glanced up and saw the youth pastor approaching. He stared straight at me, tears glistening in his own eyes.

"Hey. Don't worry. Things are gonna change for you," he said kindly.

How does he know? How does he know the hell I've

been through? "I don't want to live with my dad anymore," I cried.

"Be prepared. Things are gonna change." He gave me a hug. I sank into his embrace, grateful for the physical affection. My father had hardly ever doled out any affection growing up, and I realized how much I craved the connection. *This is a person I can trust. I have come to the right place.*

I went home that night, feeling hope for the first time in a very long while. The pastor's message replayed over and over in my mind. *All right, I don't know exactly what I'm doing here, but I really believe I'm on the right path. I believe Jesus is the missing piece I've been looking for my whole life. The enemy has used my father's abuse to beat me down, but it is not too late for me. I can still experience victory in God. Even if my circumstances do not immediately change, my heart and my attitude can.*

I continued going to church, despite my father's disapproval. One night, I walked in and found my father sprawled out on the couch, drunk and watching TV.

"Where are you going?" he barked, glancing over.

"I'm going to church, Dad. I'll be back." I paused. "I respect you because you are my dad, but that's it."

I walked out, feeling sad as I thought about my father sitting there, lost in his own little world. I cared about him, but I was tired of being tethered down by his addictions and destructive ways. *God has something more for me, and I am going to follow a new path now. Even if I don't know where that path leads, I'm going to trust in*

God to show me where to go. I believe that he is on my side, and he will fight for me.

As I began reading my Bible and praying on a regular basis, God revealed his love to me. He also revealed the deep shame I'd been carrying in my heart for years due to my pornography addiction. I felt like a dirty person for spending so much time viewing naked women. *What if people knew my dark secret? What would they think of me?*

But as I learned about God's character, I learned something astounding. He did not see me as filthy and disgusting because of my past habits. Instead, he saw me as a new creature in him. When I'd invited him into my heart and asked him to cleanse me, he'd made me new. With his help, I could overcome my addiction and wipe my slate clean.

My father sat me down one day not long after, lowering his voice to a somber tone. "Son, your mother is looking for you. She has sent you a Greyhound bus ticket." He paused, then added, "If you do go, don't bother coming back."

I sucked in my breath. My mother! After all these years! I had not seen her in more than a decade. Had she really been looking for me all this time? "I'm going to go see her," I told him with determination. "But I will come back. I'm not gonna stay, Dad."

He shrugged. "Suit yourself."

I hopped on the Greyhound the next day, my heart racing in anticipation at the idea of seeing my long-lost mother. I'd thought about her many times over the years and wondered what my life would have been like if I'd chosen her instead. Would I have slept in a warm bed, tucked in with stories every night instead of curling up in a Ford Pinto at a rest stop? Would there have been hot meals on the table instead of bare cupboards and empty stomachs? Would I perhaps have unwrapped a new toy beneath the Christmas tree like the other kids at school?

I stepped off the Greyhound bus and smoothed my best shirt, hoping I would be presentable enough for my mother. When I showed up at her door, she pulled me into a long embrace. She looked much as I remembered her, only with a few more lines around the eyes and a few more gray hairs.

"Hi, Mom," I said awkwardly.

"Oh, Rich." Behind her eyes, I saw sadness, and I wondered what sort of life she'd been living apart from me.

Over the next week, my mother told me everything. "You should know the truth, Rich," she said. "Your father and I met in a bar one night after drinking a few too many. After spending just one night together, I learned I was pregnant with you. We tried to make things work, but your father was pretty physically and mentally abusive. Finally, I could not take it anymore. I had to get out." She paused, her eyes filling with tears. "It's been a hard life, Rich."

She said my half-sister and brothers inherited some dangerous medical condition from their father, and it killed three of them. "Your older sister is all I have left." She paused again, wiping her eyes. "And you, of course."

I stared at her in disbelief, trying to absorb everything. *So I was the product of a drunken one-night stand? And my father abused you, too? And you just lost three children?* My heart went out to the woman who had lived a life 10 times harder than mine. While we'd been separated, we'd both been fighting our own battles, both victims of my father's anger and disturbing ways.

"You know, Rich, I've always felt really guilty about not fighting for you in court. I wish I could take that all back. But if I'd taken you in, I would not have been able to care for you properly, because I had to focus all my time on my sick children. So you see … that's the story." Her voice trailed off, and for a moment, she was lost in her own world of grief.

"Wow. I don't even know what to say." I sat there, still too shocked to respond. At last, I spoke up. "So, you tried to look for me over the years?"

"Of course. But your dad was always on the move, making it impossible for me to track you down."

So you did try, Mom. "Well, this is a lot to take in," I told her. "I'm glad I came, though."

My mother introduced me to my sister, who was now grown with daughters of her own. I enjoyed meeting my nieces, a bit saddened that I'd never known this part of my family. After a week, I decided to go back to my father. As much as I disliked living with him, I knew I didn't belong at my mother's. We were like two strangers, both trying to wade through a sea of hurt, lies, dysfunction and pain. I hopped back on the Greyhound and went home.

When I returned, my father delivered some surprising news. "I'm moving, Rich. Gonna head up to North Dakota and start a new life there. I paid the rent on this apartment for six months, so you can live here if you want."

I stared at him in disbelief. "Wait a second. So I'm 16 years old, and you're telling me that you are leaving me? That's it?"

My father nodded. "Yep."

"Wow. Okay, well, have a nice life." *I can't believe it! I come back, and just like that, my father decides to split! I'm not even a legal adult yet. What does he expect me to do?*

A week later, my father took off. I decided to stay in the apartment until I could figure out what to do next. I'd have to find a job, finish school and figure out how to make my own way in the world. I was the man of the house now, whether I liked it or not.

I continued going to church, grateful for my new friends and my youth pastor there. For the first time, I felt like I belonged somewhere, like I had a true family who cared about me.

As the six months' rent on the apartment neared expiration, I realized I needed to act fast. I began praying, asking God to provide a place for me to live. At 16, I knew there was no way I could make it on my own. But since inviting God into my life, I had learned to rely on him for all things. My youth pastor reminded us that God had already mapped out all the days of our life, and we did not need to worry. He would take care of us.

I have something better for you, I sensed God saying to me. *Just hang in there.*

I confided in my youth pastor's mother about my situation. "In just a few weeks, I'm not gonna have a place to live," I told her. "I don't know what I'm going to do."

"You are going to come live with us," she said with a smile.

"Really?" I stammered, shocked by her offer.

"Really."

Wow, God, you totally answered my prayers! Thank you!

I moved in with the family, and they treated me like one of their own. Within no time, I realized it was the best decision I ever could have made. They gave me my own room, complete with a warm bed and crisp, clean sheets. There were hot meals for dinner, prayers before bedtime and plenty of laughter to go around. Best of all, we talked. I didn't realize how lonely I'd been growing up with my father, but now I understood how a true family worked. Families shared one another's burdens, rejoicing together when something great happened and crying together after a tough day. I had never experienced that before.

My youth pastor's mother became like a surrogate mother to me, and I valued her wisdom and direction. I spent the next year and a half at her home, letting her love on me. I realized how detrimental it had been to grow up without a mother's nurturing spirit. But God had given me one when I needed it most, and I would be forever grateful.

When I was 17, I learned the painful truth about my father's finances. He had been hawking the food stamps we received every month, selling $100 worth of the stamps for as little as $20 cash to folks on the streets. He had then taken that money and headed down to the liquor store to stock up on his booze. All those years, he'd been using me as a free ticket to support his alcohol addiction.

The news stung, and I began to grow angry again. *How could my father have done something like that? I never want to be like him!* I decided vehemently. But in my anger, I remembered my youth pastor's words. *There is someone who does not want you to have victory. You have victory in Christ, Rich. You are a new creation in him.*

I landed a great job in the carpet industry, repairing, installing and cleaning carpet. Meanwhile, my buddy and I started a Christian rap group. Though I had followed my father all over Northern California as he pursued his gypsy lifestyle, I had never truly had my own adventure. I grew excited as we toured from city to city, setting up at churches and worshipping God through our music. For the first time in my life, I was doing something I loved — something I was good at. Something with purpose.

One weekend, we set up at a church in Concord. When I walked into the church, I spotted a woman laying out a display of her ministry. She worked with a ministry on a Native American reservation. The display intrigued me because of my heritage, so I sauntered up to introduce myself.

"Hi, I'm Violet," she said warmly, shaking my hand. "Nice to meet you."

Out of the corner of my eye, I spotted a beautiful girl. I introduced myself to her as well and learned her name was Kari.

"We're from a reservation in Oregon," her mother explained. "We're here to share about our ministry."

"Oh, cool. I actually lived on a reservation when I was really young," I told them. "I'm in a rap group, and we're here to perform tonight."

I went on stage, and my buddy and I did five or six songs. Afterward, I approached Kari's mother as she packed up. "Hey, would it be okay if I wrote your daughter once you get back to Oregon?"

"Sure."

Unable to get Kari out of my mind, I wrote her a letter after I got home, asking her to tell me a bit more about herself. When a letter arrived in the mailbox shortly after, I could not tear it open fast enough. We wrote back and forth for the next several months, getting to know one another. After her family agreed we could see each other, I made the eight-hour trek up to Oregon to visit her twice a month. Within no time, I was falling hard.

Since living with my youth pastor's family, I had begun praying for a family of my own someday. I had never had a stable situation, but I knew that I had much to offer. I dreamed of having a wife and children and being able to provide for them. Was God answering my prayers and giving me the woman of my dreams in a girl like Kari?

"You have to hold your job for at least six months before I can marry you," Kari told me firmly.

I was happy to oblige. I loved my job and looked forward to providing for my future wife. After spending my entire childhood living in poverty and disarray, I was determined to create a stable home for my family someday. My adoptive mother had instilled a good work ethic and values in me, reminding me that a godly man worked hard to take care of his household. My father had been my only earthly example for many years, but after being involved in church, I now had plenty of other men to emulate.

After several more long-distance trips, I asked Kari to marry me. We wed in 1995, with my entire church family sitting in the audience as our guests of honor. It was a beautiful day I would never forget. Kari loved me, but most importantly, she loved God. At last, I had someone to share my life with. And I could not have chosen a more perfect companion.

Three years into our marriage, Kari gave birth to a beautiful little girl, Heidi. As thrilled as I was to be a father, a bit of me was frightened at the prospect. *What if I don't do a good job? Worse yet, what if I end up like my father?* I did not feel equipped to take on such a big role. But as I prayed, God reminded me that I only needed to look to him. He would show me how to do things right.

Kari and I got more involved at our church and began

working with the youth. I played the drums for worship, and Kari played the keyboard. Neither of us was very good, but the kids didn't seem to mind. I had a real heart for the teens, as only a few years before, I'd been a lonely, troubled adolescent myself. But a youth pastor had given me a hug and told me things would get better, and his words of affirmation had changed my life. I hoped to do the same for some hurting kid.

Kari gave birth to another little girl, Diana, when Heidi was 2. As our little family expanded, I thanked God for his provision. Sometimes, as I glanced around the dinner table, I felt as though my heart might explode with happiness. *This is everything I prayed for and dreamed about but never imagined could come true, God. Thank you!*

One day, Heidi misbehaved, and I decided to correct her. I began spanking her over and over, growing angrier with every swat. Tears filled her eyes, and her little lip began to quiver. My anger swelled, and I struggled to contain it. Suddenly, all of my father's abuse rushed back to me at once. My mind snapped to the many times he'd whipped off his belt and chased me around the room, to the nights he'd kicked me out of bed and punched me on the ground, to the curse words that had flown out of his mouth in his rage, to the bruises I tried to hide the morning after he beat me down.

Dad, how could you have?

I stopped spanking my daughter and fell to my knees, sobbing like never before. *I don't want to be like my father. I don't want to repeat his abuse. Oh, God, help me. Remove this bad spirit from me, and replace it with your peace. Let the vicious cycle end now.*

I scooped up my daughter and pulled her into a long embrace. "I'm sorry, sweetie. Oh, Daddy's so sorry. Will you forgive me?"

Little Heidi nodded, and we both wiped our tears.

Victory, Rich. Remember, God wants you to have victory. Your childhood lifestyle of abuse, pornography and poverty does not have to be repeated. What Satan meant for evil, God will use for good. He has restored your life.

We welcomed a third little girl, Hillary, when our middle daughter was 2. During one of her routine checkups as a toddler, we learned that she had scoliosis. After several X-rays, the doctors confirmed that her neck was unusually crooked, and she would need several surgeries to correct it. Kari and I began to pray, asking God for direction. We faced a major ordeal, not just physically, but financially as well.

"God, we give this one to you. We trust you with our little girl. Please show us what to do," we prayed.

A nurse gave us the number to Shriner's Hospital in Sacramento, an esteemed, non-profit hospital. We called, and they reviewed our situation and agreed to operate. Hillary would need rod extensions in her back and another surgery on her neck. It was a precarious situation, but if we did not go through with the operation, she might not be able to walk properly someday.

The day the doctors wheeled Hillary back for surgery was one of the hardest moments of my entire life. As a father, I wanted to run after my little girl and throw my arms around her.

"Daddy! Daddy!" Hillary cried, tears streaming down her cheeks.

"You're gonna be just fine, baby. Just fine," I assured her, my own tears coming in a flood. *Oh, please, God, watch over her.*

The doctors inserted several pins in her skull and prepared her for surgery. I paced the waiting room, praying and hoping for good news. When at last they emerged and told us the surgery had been successful, my wife and I rejoiced. Our little girl had a long road ahead of her with more surgeries to come, but we'd gotten the hardest part out of the way. She was going to be okay.

❧❧❧

"Wow, look at that! Did you see that cartwheel?" I turned to Kari and laughed as little Hillary bounded across the yard.

"Amazing!" Kari cheered, clapping as Hillary raced toward us.

After a total of eight surgeries, Hillary's spine was better, but there was still more that needed to be done. Despite our hardships, we continued to thank God. He had taken care of our little girl, as well as our finances, and we now had a future gymnast on our hands.

STRUCK

Now in our mid-30s, Kari and I are enjoying life to the fullest. After attending the same church for years, we began to see a need for a better youth group for our kids. I began praying about switching churches but kept prolonging the decision, as I was involved playing the drums and doing other ministry work. But it was my adoptive mother who helped make the decision easy for me one day.

"You need to get those kids in a church where they can grow," she told me.

We landed at Celebration Church in Fairfield and never looked back. At Celebration, my family and I feel right at home. The people are welcoming, the teaching is great and there are plenty of activities for my growing kids. Kari and I have enjoyed supporting the youth group our daughters attend, and I sometimes play in the worship band. Just like my adoptive family, I've found yet another place where I belong, and I could not ask for a better group of people in my life.

Six years ago, my father moved back to Northern California. He calls me once in a while, trying to be a friend to me. Though he has never told me he is sorry for the hell he dragged me through, I have forgiven him in my heart. I know that he envies the life I now have — a stable job I've held for nearly 20 years, three beautiful girls, a lovely wife and a nice home. I try to remind him that he, too, can have a good life. But it all begins with surrendering everything and inviting Jesus into his heart.

Years ago, I reestablished a relationship with my

biological mother as well. Now in her mid-70s, she continues to lead a difficult life. She has told me she is sorry for the choices she has made, and I have forgiven her as well.

My grandmother passed away six years ago after a long battle with dementia. She made it clear her entire life that my father was never to have a dime of her money when she died. Though it hurt me for years that my relatives did not stand up for me in the midst of my father's abuse, I now have a better understanding of why they remained silent. My grandmother had endured two abusive marriages herself, and she knew all too well the repercussions of trying to fight back. I now understand that look in her eyes when she watched my father whip out his belt and beat me. She bore bruises of her own, and she'd hidden them from the world for years.

Today, as I watch my daughters play in our backyard, I can't help but beam with happiness. As a young boy, fighting for sleep in a beat-up Ford Pinto at a rest stop, I wondered if there was life beyond my unhappiness. As I hopped from school to school, watching as other kids scooped up Christmas gifts and new clothes, I wondered if I'd ever have anything nice of my own. After years of abuse, I wondered if I'd ever claw my way out of my destructive, depressing situation.

But I now know that God saw me the whole time. He saw me in my grief and held me when I cried. He saw the boy with the hand-me-down shoes, whose empty stomach grumbled as he huddled on a cold cot in a dark city shelter. He saw the boy who flipped through those magazines, emulating his father's behavior as he peeked at the scantily clad women. And he saw my shame that followed, the years I spent wondering if I'd ever be enough, wondering how anyone would ever find me loveable.

And then he rescued me.

God pulled me out of my loneliness and pain and placed me in a real family who loved me unconditionally. He plugged me into a church where I learned to grow in my new faith. He turned my ugly, broken life into something good — something beautiful. I never imagined I'd be where I am today. At one time, I had no hope. But today, I have hope because of Jesus Christ. Without him, I am nothing. He is my provider, my healer, my guide and my best friend. He has made my heart full and given me reason to live. And I could not ask for more. In him, I am finally home.

CONCLUSION

Wow! What amazing stories from people who chose to *get up*. Every one of these individuals had a common theme that helped them through the most difficult situations of life. That theme was: "I couldn't get up by myself; I needed someone's help." The Bible tells us in II Corinthians 4:7-9: "But we have this treasure in earthen vessels, that the excellence of the **power may be of God and not of us.** We are hard-pressed on every side, yet not crushed; we are perplexed, but not in despair; persecuted, but not forsaken; **struck down, but not destroyed.**"

We've all been struck down, but we don't have to be destroyed! God has a better plan for our lives. The individuals in this book found their power in God's plan and not themselves. If we could wish it better or hope it better, we would — but we can't. That's why we need God's help.

Your life really can change. It is possible to become a new person. The seven stories in this book prove positively that people right here in Fairfield have stopped dying and started living. Whether you've been struck by abuse, broken promises, shattered dreams or suffocating addictions, the resounding answer is … "Yes! You can become a new person."

I want to encourage you that God has amazing things in store for your life if you would just give him a chance. I know you won't be sorry. The situations you are in may seem overwhelming right now. But God is greater than anything that comes against you.

All of the people you just read about made the most important decision any of us will ever make. They surrendered their lives to Jesus Christ. So, how can you make that same decision?

1. Know that God loves you no matter what you've done or where you've been. "Who shall separate us from the love of Christ? Shall tribulation, or distress, or persecution, or famine, or nakedness, or peril, or sword? Yet in all these things we are more than conquerors through him who loved us. For I am persuaded that neither death nor life, nor angels nor principalities nor powers, nor things present nor things to come, nor height nor depth, nor any other created thing shall be able to separate us from the love of God which is in Christ Jesus our Lord" (Romans 8:35, 37-39).

2. You can receive God's love through accepting his son, Jesus, who died on the cross so we could be forgiven of our wrongdoings and have eternal life in heaven. "But God shows and clearly proves his (own) love for us by the fact that while we were still sinners, Christ (the Messiah, the Anointed One) died for us" (Romans 5:8).

"For God so loved the world that he gave his only begotten son, that whoever believes in him should not perish but have everlasting life" (John 3:16).

CONCLUSION

How do you accept this love? The Bible tells us "that if you confess with your mouth the Lord Jesus and believe in your heart that God has raised him from the dead, you will be saved. For with the heart one believes unto righteousness, and with the mouth confession is made unto salvation" (Romans 10:9-10).

It's that easy! Just confess your sins, believe in your heart and you are saved!

Pray this prayer, and if you mean it, then you are starting the greatest journey of your life.

Lord Jesus. I invite you into my life now. I confess that I am a sinner and my sin has separated me from God. I ask that you would forgive me of all my sins and wipe my slate clean. Today I start a new life with you as my Lord. I want you to come live in me now and give me power to overcome all of these obstacles in my life. I know I could never do this on my own. I need you. Thank you for dying for my sins. Thank you for rising again on the third day. And thank you for giving me a new life. In Jesus' name. Amen.

3. Find a good church and friends that will help you get up!

You may not understand everything you just prayed and read. That's why God gave us pastors and churches to help us in our journey. I would like to personally invite you to Celebration Church this week. At Celebration, you will find real people, with real problems, who have made big mistakes, failed and are far from perfect. But you will also find that they are genuine friends who love God, each other and are way better together than they are by themselves. Come check us out! You'll be glad you did. We are casual, so come as you are.

Pastor Vernon Barker
Celebration Church

We would love for you to join us at Celebration Church!

We meet at
1837 Blossom Avenue, Fairfield, CA 94533.

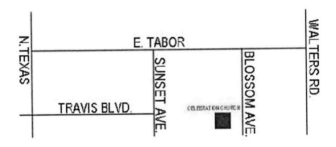

Service Times:
Sunday - Main Service: 10 a.m.
Youth Service: 5 p.m.
Tuesday - Basic Believers Class: 7 p.m.

For more information or directions:
www.celebrationfairfield.com
Phone: 707.422.5250
Fax: 707.425.5555
E-mail: celebration.church@sbcglobal.net

For more information on reaching your city with stories from your church, go to www.testimonybooks.com.

GOOD CATCH
PUBLISHING

Did one of these stories touch you?
Did one of these real people move you to tears?
Tell us (and them) about it on our Facebook page at
www.facebook.com/GoodCatchPublishing.